ro/a

IN THE TRACKS OF BUDDHISM

M
A
N
D
A
L
A

Frithjof Schuon was described by T. S. Eliot as the most impressive writer in the field of comparative religion he had encountered. He studied Arabic and Arabic calligraphy before exploring Islam and Buddhism in North Africa, India and Turkey.

Frithjof Schuon is the author of *Understanding Islam* (Mandala, 1986).

IN THE TRACKS
OF BUDDHISM

FRITHJOF SCHUON

Translated from the French
by
Marco Pallis

M A N D A L A

UNWIN PAPERBACKS

London   Boston   Sydney   Wellington

First published in Great Britain by George Allen & Unwin Ltd, 1968
Reprinted by Unwin® Paperbacks, an imprint of Unwin Hyman
Limited, in 1989.

Unwin Hyman Limited
15–17 Broadwick Street
London W1V 1FP

Allen & Unwin Inc.
9 Winchester Terrace, Winchester, MA 01890, USA

Allen & Unwin Pty Ltd
8 Napier Street, North Sydney, NSW 2060, Australia

Allen & Unwin New Zealand Pty Ltd in association with the
Port Nicholson Press
Compusales Building, 75 Ghuznee Street, Wellington, New Zealand

ISBN 0–04–440458–1

British Library CIP data available on request

Printed and bound in Great Britain by Cox & Wyman Ltd, Reading.

TRANSLATOR'S PREFACE

THOSE who are already acquainted with Frithjof Schuon's writings will know that Buddhist themes have frequently figured there, side by side with references to the other great traditions, by way of illustrating the manifold phases of spiritual life both at the theoretical and the 'operative' level, as realized by men. The present book marks the first occasion when a whole volume by this author has been specifically allotted to consideration of that form of spirituality which stems from the Buddha; it is the third work of this type to come from his pen, the two others being *Language of the Self* (Ganesh, Madras 1959) which treats of Hinduism and, more recently, *Understanding Islam* (Allen and Unwin 1963): it was the success of the latter work which in the first place suggested the idea of a companion volume devoted to Buddhism, one in which the author's most important Buddhist commentaries would be assembled and edited to form a self-contained whole. In fact, about two thirds of the present work, carefully revised, rearranged and amplified, has come from a collection, published by Flammarion in 1961 and entitled *Images de l'Esprit;* to this the author has added some entirely fresh material expressly composed for the present book and including its final chapter on the Six Transcendent Virtues (the *pāramitās*) wherein the Buddhist wisdom is summed up and through which it may be got to flower in a human life of sanctity; Enlightenment is their fully ripened fruit.

Something may appropriately be said here about the author's own attitude to Buddhism, as expressed in this and other works: if his illustrations have been largely, though not exclusively, drawn from Mahāyānist and notably from Japanese sources with which he is especially familiar, this must on no account be read as evidence that he underrates the authority or spiritual spontaneity of the *Theravāda* – he says quite plainly that, for him, all the schools of traditional Buddhism, across their differences of emphasis and expression and even their occasional conflicts, are Buddhism and nothing else. Each in its own way voices one and the same spiritual principle; indeed their very variety serves to bring out a particular property of

7

the Buddhist genius (one might also have said, of the Indian genius) namely its power to adapt the essential message to the temperamental needs of differing types of men, speaking to all in the kind of language they will best understand; in particular the diffusion of Buddhism among the Yellow races has resulted in a remarkable flowering of schools and doctrines. Buddhism is *par excellence* the religion of *upāyas*, provisional means, and these have to be as variable as the beings whose spiritual food they are meant to supply; but all have the same purpose in view, namely an awakening of *prajnā*, the liberating wisdom transcending all names and forms. In this matter the author gladly takes his stand beside the great Japanese saint Hōnen when he declares, after enumerating the principal schools of his time with their characteristics, that:

'What they all say is exactly what the Sūtras and Shastras say and corresponds to the golden words of Nyorai (Gautama) himself who, according to men's varying capacity, taught them at one time one thing and at another another, as circumstances required . . . If we but attend to our religious practices as the Sūtras teach they will all help us to pass safely over the sea of birth and death to the other shore. If we act according to the Law, we shall attain Enlightenment . . . The one thing to do is to put the principles into practice, because they all teach the way of deliverance from the dread bondage.'

To turn to a purely practical matter of literary dialectic: the author wishes mention to be made of certain expedients of wording commonly employed in his texts; in order to make apparent the reasons behind their use, it is best to quote his own words, taken from a similar context elsewhere:

'We regret the very frequent use of capitals as also of inverted commas, but we are compelled to do this, partly because of loose habits, inconsistencies and linguistic misuses on the part of many writers today and partly in order to compensate for the imprecision of a language that has become somewhat outworn, as the case may be. To give one example: if it be conventional to write "the gods" with small letters this is because the gods, put in the plural, are always assumed to be false; but, apart from the fact that some writers go as far as to write "the Saints" with a capital, one does not see why small letters should be used when referring to "Gods" one believes to be true.'

The reader should find no difficulty in perceiving why one of the above-mentioned expedients has been used in any given case.

One thing that could occasion surprise to some readers is the occurrence, between the covers of this book, of considerable passages the subject-matter of which does not, at first sight, seem to come under a strictly Buddhist label. The reason for these digressions, which are more apparent than real, is because one of the purposes the author constantly has in mind is to relate the traditional teachings to present situations: his dialectic is largely conditioned by this aim. Neither in expounding Buddhism nor the doctrines of any other religion does he set out to provide a text-book, complete with theoretical, historical, ethical and other data systematically arranged and presented. Rather does he handle his subject on free lines, focussing attention on whatever will serve to illustrate the point of the moment; his treatment of the subject in question has something of the character of a series of discontinuous (though invisibly connected) tableaux; the form of the title chosen for this book is in keeping with such a technique. This method moreover is not alien to the spirit of Buddhism, whose teachings are also able to become a touchstone of discernment in regard to many contemporary beliefs and assumptions examined in these pages – a mirror in which they may be viewed and there caused to display their true colours. The Buddhist wisdom, like the Christian or Hindu or Islamic wisdom moreover, provides all the necessary criteria for this purpose, so that the apparent digressions will explain themselves in the light of what has just been said.

The foregoing considerations now bring us up against another question, not foreign to the writing of this book, one that concerns the Buddhist world in a rather peculiar way: the reproach (intended as a compliment!) has been imputed to Buddhism by more than one present day propagandist on its behalf that its teachings and those of modern empirical science, especially in the psychological and sociological fields, are perfectly reconcilable; one has even heard it said that the Buddha's teachings and those of Marxism are not incompatible (such is evidently not the opinion of the Chinese Marxists, however). The motives behind this kind of statement are apparent enough: partly there is the wish to make Buddhism sound acceptable in modern ears in opposition to Christianity or the other 'theistic' religions: and partly – this applies especially to Orientals who, thanks to a Westernised education, are no longer quite sure where they belong – by the wish to appear in line with 'twentieth century thinking' at all costs. The only remedy for this state of mind with its accompanying susceptibility to every kind of subversive suggestion is to cultivate deliberately ('mindfully' in the Buddhist sense) a habit of rigorous discrimination extending both to the intellectual sphere in all its departments and even to the day-to-day sphere of personal behaviour. Some of the detailed discussions in the pages to follow are well calculated to foster this kind of habitual vigilance.

Part II of this book calls for a few special remarks inasmuch as it treats of the ideas and symbolism and also of the mythology of Shintō, the native tradition that preceded Buddhism in Japan and has continued to exert an influence in conjunction with the latter down to our time: the outcome of this association is the Japanese civilization in all its originality and beauty. No one who reads this book will fail to notice how dear to the heart of the author that civilization is; he himself mentions an episode of his boyhood when the seed of that love first implanted itself in his breast. As was said before, however, this strong sympathy for one form of Buddhism and for the people who are attached to that form has never operated, with the author, to the detriment of other traditional forms of like validity.

Very few Europeans have much idea of what Shintō is about; in fact many people in the West feel a certain prejudice against it inasmuch as its ethical prescriptions, especially those relating to chivalry and honour, were shamelessly exploited in the period that followed the Meiji revolution by those whose interest it was to turn the Japanese sense of loyalty into an instrument of a modern (therefore essentially Western and profane) nationalism; the disasters of our time proceed from there. To correct this false impression, a just exposition of what Shintō really stands for was much needed; it is therefore not unfitting that a book about that Buddhism which, for Shintō, provided its historical and metaphysical complement should now also serve as a setting for this task of redress.

In conclusion, fitting acknowledgement should be made for the skilled assistance offered by three of the translator's friends, Mrs M. H. Robins, Richard Nicholson and William Stoddart, who either helped with putting certain chapters into English or with the exacting work of correcting the translated text and clearing up doubtful points of various kinds; thanks to them, the work of preparing this volume was rendered that much lighter.

MARCO PALLIS

CONTENTS

PART I

IN THE TRACKS OF BUDDHISM

CHAPTER I

ORIGINALITY OF BUDDHISM

WHOEVER sets out to define a spiritual phenomenon situated in the almost heavenly era of the great Revelations has to beware of assessing it according to the impoverished categories of later ages or, still worse, those belonging to the inbuilt profanity of the 'free-thinking' world. Buddhism, which many have tried to reduce to the level of a commonplace philosophical empiricism, is anything but a purely human ideology; were it such, its quality as a way of enlightenment or salvation would be unintelligible. To deny the celestial character of Sākyamuni and his Message is after all tantamount to saying that there can be effects without a cause, and this remark moreover holds good for all inspired Messengers and all sacred institutions. The Buddha, despite certain appearances, was not a 'reformer' in the current sense of the word — which implies heterodoxy – and could not be such; all that weighs with a reformer in that sense is to bring back the religion to which he adheres, or thinks he adheres, to its 'primitive purity'; this task he tries to accomplish by rejecting essential elements rather like a man who, wishing to refer a tree back to its root, would saw off all its branches and even its trunk. The would-be reformer, whose idea of 'purity' is entirely external and in no wise transcendent, fails to perceive that the branches normally and legitimately contain the root and even the seed and that the sap is the same throughout the tree down to its smallest shoot and that every organism has its laws of growth, determined not only by its own particular nature but also by its medium of expansion; such a person forgets that time as such is irreversible and that the qualitative differences of temporal cycles necessitate readaptations, for any given tradition, in a more explicit or more differentiated sense just as happens with the tree, analogically speaking, the branches of which are more complex than the trunk. The Buddha, direct manifestation of the Spirit, had both the power and the right to place himself outside the tradition in which he was born; he had no call to concern himself with the purity of Hinduism nor did he think of reforming the latter; the pre-existing frameworks, which were moreover and humanly speaking decadent in his time, represented for him no more than formalism as such; they stood for a pharisaism whereof 'the letter' kills.

Be it noted, however, that here the reference is to formalism and pharisaism, not to form and orthodoxy; it is a question of abuses and not of the things themselves that have been abused; this must be remembered even while saying that the Buddhist perspective, as such, had no need to make this particular distinction in regard to Hinduism. In any case, orthodox reformers have also existed, such as Tsongkhapa in Tibetan Buddhism and, in the West, SS. John of the Cross and Teresa of Avila, not forgetting Savonarola; but in their case there never had been a question of invalidating any principle of the tradition, indeed quite the contrary.

The first question to be put concerning any doctrine or tradition is that of its intrinsic orthodoxy; that is to say one must know whether that tradition is consonant, not necessarily with such another traditionally orthodox perspective, but simply with Truth. As far as Buddhism is concerned, we will not ask ourselves therefore whether it agrees with the letter of the *Veda* or if its 'non-theism' (not 'atheism') is reconcilable, in its expression, with the Semitic theism or any other, but only whether Buddhism is true in itself; which means, if the answer be affirmative, that it will agree with the Vedic spirit and that its non-theism will express the truth, or a sufficient aspect of the truth, whereof theism provides another possible expression, opportune in the world governed by it. In point of fact, a particular spiritual perspective is commonly discoverable somewhere within the framework of a tradition that seems to exclude it; thus, theism reappears in a certain sense in the framework of Buddhism despite its characteristic non-theism, both in a diffused form as the countless Buddhas and Bodhisattvas manifested in, or revealed to, the worlds and to whom worship is due, and also, to cite one particularly striking example, in the cult of the Buddha Amitābha, infinite Light, associated with the Pure Land schools of China and Japan. Conversely, the Buddhist 'non-theism' reappears in its turn with the conception of the 'impersonal Essence' of the Divinity pertaining to all the monotheistic esotericisms: from the above examples it will be seen that religious frameworks have nothing exclusive about them; rather always is it a question of emphasis or spiritual economy.

The not infrequent employment, by the Buddha, of terms proper to the Brahmanical theism clearly shows that the Buddhist perspective has nothing in common with atheism properly so called; it is a perversity of some Western propagandists on behalf of Buddhism as also of some Orientals wishful of appearing in line with modern 'humanism' to have confused the issue in this respect. 'Extinction' (*Nirvāna*) or 'the Void' is but 'God' subjectivised, as a state of realization; 'God' is but the Void objectively regarded, as Principle. If Buddhists, except when taking up the standpoint of Mercy, abstain from objectivising the Void or the Self, this is because they have nothing to ask of it, given their own anti-individualist point of view; if nevertheless there are certain 'dimensions' where things appear otherwise, this is because the 'objective aspect' of Reality is too much in the nature of things to pass unperceived and without being turned to account on occasion.

All that has just been said means implicitly that Buddhism, inasmuch as it is a characteristic perspective and independently of its various modes, answers to a necessity: it could not but come to be, given that a non-anthropomorphic, impersonal and 'static' consideration of the Infinite is in itself a possibility; such a perspective had therefore to be manifested at a cyclic moment and in human surroundings that rendered it opportune, for wherever the receptacle is, there the content imposes itself. People have sometimes remarked on the fact that the Buddhist perspective is not distinguishable in any very essential way from such and such doctrines found in Hinduism; this is true up to a point, being all the more likely inasmuch as Hinduism is characterized by an uncommon wealth of doctrines and methods; but it would be wrong to infer from this that Buddhism does not represent as spontaneous and autonomous a reality as do the other great Revelations; what may be said is that Buddhism is something like a Hinduism universalized, just as Christianity and Islam, each in its own way, are a Judaism rendered universal and therefore detached from its particular ethnic environment and thus made accessible to men of all manner of racial origins. Buddhism in a way extracted from Hinduism its yogic sap, not through a borrowing, be it understood, but through a divinely inspired remanifestation, and it imparted to this substance an expression that was simplified in certain respects, but at the same time fresh and powerfully original.

This is proved, among other things, by Buddhist art, of which the prototypes may doubtless be discerned in the yogic postures common to Indian sacred iconography or again in the dance which, for its part, is like an intermediary between *yoga* and the temple statuary: Buddhist art – and here one is thinking chiefly of images of the Buddha – seems to have extracted from Hindu art, not such and such a particular symbolism, but its contemplative essence. The plastic arts of India evolve in a last analysis round the human body in its postures of recollection; in Buddhism the image of this body and this visage has become a symbol of extraordinary fecundity and a means of grace of unsurpassable power and nobility, to which the genius of the Yellow race has added, on the basis of the Indian prototypes, something not far short of a fresh dimension; fresh, not from the point of view of the symbolism as such, but from that of expression. It is through this artistic crystallization that what Buddhism comprises of absoluteness and therefore also of universality is most vividly displayed to an outside observer. The sacred image transmits a message of serenity: the Buddhist Dharma is not a passionate struggle against passion, it dissolves passion from within, through contemplation. The lotus, supporting the Buddha, is the nature of things, the calm and pure fatality of existence, of its illusion and finally of its disappearance; but it is also the luminous centre of *Māyā* whence arises Nirvāna become man.

From the doctrinal point of view the great originality of Buddhism is to consider the Divine, not in relation to its cosmic manifestations as ontological cause and anthropomorphic personification, but rather in relation to its acosmic and anonymous character, as supra-existential 'state' which then will appear as Voidness (*shūnyatā*) from the point of view of the false plenitude of existence (*samsāra*); the latter is the realm of 'thirst' (*trishnā*). By this view of things stress is laid on the unconditional character of the divine Goodness, or rather of the 'nirvānic Grace' projected, as this is, through a myriad of Buddhas and Bodhisattvas into the round of transmigration and even down to the hells; faith in the infinite mercy of the Buddha, himself an illusory appearance of the beatific Void, already constitutes a grace or a gift. Salvation consists in coming out of the infernal circle of 'concordant actions and reactions'; seen from this standpoint, morality appears like a provisional and fragmentary thing and even as inoperative in the sight of the Absolute, if only because it is itself involved in the indefinite chain of acts and the existential fruit of acts. Forms such as Zen and the Pure Land doctrine of Amitābha's 'original vow' are particularly effective in allowing one to sense the subtle relationships, made up of imponderables and paradoxes, at once separating and connecting the world of Transmigration and Extinction, Samsāra and Nirvāna.

*

The Buddhist 'non-theism' offers the advantage of avoiding an impression of an interested God; this advantage is evidently a relative and conditional one, but it has its importance for the sake of certain mentalities. As Buddhists see things, moreover, the religious dissensions of the monotheist world are bound up with a dogmatic and anthropomorphic theism as such; no God without a party, no party without struggle against another party. Needless to say, this view represents but a partial truth, for which the theistic conception compensates by its own intrinsic values.

If it be admitted that, as Christ said, 'the Kingdom of Heaven is within you', there is no logical cause to reproach Buddhism for conceiving the Divine Principle in this respect alone. 'The Void' or 'Extinction' is God (supra-ontological Reality and Being inwardly regarded) within ourselves; not in our thoughts or in our ego, be it understood, but starting out from that 'geometrical point' within us whereby we remain attached mysteriously to the Infinite.

The so-called Buddhist atheism consists in a refusal to objectivize or to exteriorize dogmatically the 'God within'. Nevertheless, such an objectivizing does occur on occasion in a 'provisional' sense and as an instrument of method (*upāya*) as, for example, in the merciful message of the Buddha Amitābha previously mentioned; a fact which, to be even possible, proves precisely this, namely that Buddhism is in no wise atheistical, in the privative sense of the word. The symbolism of the Pure Land or of other similar paradisial abodes would not be possible in Buddhism if those 'Buddha-lands' were not reconcilable with the intrinsic nature of Extinction, Nirvāna, or in other words if they did not describe in manifested, exteriorized and diversified mode the ineffable Reality of the Self.

The fact that Buddhism is founded, dialectically and methodically, on the experience of suffering has given rise to criticisms of a kind to be expected in our time, such as the accusation of being 'pessimistic', 'purely negative', 'against nature' and so forth; and this makes it necessary to denounce a double error, firstly that suffering is meaningless and secondly that suffering can be, not only transcended as Buddhism teaches us, but also abolished on its own level, the level of desire and worldly life. For anyone who views things in this way, all religions will evidently appear as attempts at 'resignation' or 'flight from life': but the inanity and hypocrisy of these reproaches stare one in the face, since those who express them, just like other people, are compelled to resign themselves in the face of certain happenings and to flee from others: they have to accept fatalities such as birth, old age, death, existence itself and they run away, just like the religious believer they affect to despise, before the forces of nature that threaten them and which they are incapable of resisting. The only difference is that these people do not know that certain things are simply fatalities whereas other things are mortal dangers from which it is nevertheless possible to escape and which the believer does escape from in fact. It is self-evident that one has no motive for resigning oneself to a situation that one believes can and should be changed, and one also has no reason to flee from a peril of which one is quite unaware; however, it will doubtless always be easy to disguise one's own ignorance in the form of an icy and embittered moralism that gives itself heroic airs, according to the taste of the time. If the 'zeal for bitterness leads to hell', as St Benedict said, this is because it is founded in pride; and in fact there is no worse form of pride than the insolent presupposition according to which all the Prophets, all the Sages, all the Saints were simpletons, a fact of which Mr X or Mr Y – who alone are 'heroic' and 'sincere' so it would seem! – have at long last come to take cognizance, after thousands of years gone waste.

Buddhism is not 'pessimistic', it is simply aware of the deepest nature of things.

CHAPTER II

MESSAGE AND MESSENGER

In order to understand Buddhism in all its vast and varied extension, it is necessary to distinguish, in the Buddha himself, between his teaching and his being: his teaching, which is that of suffering and the way of deliverance from suffering; his being, which first of all is manifested in the visible presence of the Buddha in the world and subsequently is crystallized in his sacred image and rendered more explicit in the sermons of the latter part of his life, those on which the Mahāyāna is founded.

What here is meant by 'the Buddha's being' refers to the merciful and at the same time to the esoteric contents of his Message; this feature is moreover discernible already in Theravādic Buddhism despite the fact that the latter remains closed to the specifically Mahāyānic *sūtras;* the same thing would be apparent even if our only evidence consisted of the sacred figure of the Buddha, the cult of which is prevalent in all countries of the Buddhist East without exception.

From a purely logical point of view, it might be objected that there is a contradiction between the basic teaching, which rejects any cult even of the person of the Blessed One, (the Dharma or Law alone being regarded as the agent of salvation) and all those other elements which, on the contrary, centre round that person, his body and his name, whereof the spiritual heritage is dominant in Northern Buddhism; but in fact, both the above points of view are equally legitimate since, if it be true to say that logically the Message takes precedence over the Messenger, it is also true that the latter is identified with the former and that the personal instrument of Revelation himself possesses the saving virtue of the Message; a certain relative opposition between two such complementary dimensions of one and the same truth is in the nature of things. In this connection one may recall the following saying of Christ: 'It is expedient for you that I go away' as well as the fact that neither the Eucharistic Sacrifice nor the descent of the Holy Spirit would be conceivable without the prior departure of Jesus: the point one is trying to make here is that the Buddha while still living on earth is able to reject all personalism, but that the Buddha once 'departed' must become all the more 'present' for us; Law and Person, Message and Messenger henceforth are one and only.

For a proper appreciation of Buddhism and its teaching the following point has to be borne in mind: this perspective is founded *a priori* on the concrete fact of human experience in general under its most immediate and tangible aspect, with provisional omission of every element that does not enter directly into that experience. Now the Buddha, as spokesman of this perspective, could not exteriorize his own nature as vehicle of salvation on the very plane of a Law that apparently confers, by the logic of things, the whole initiative of deliverance on man himself. This saving power of the Buddhic nature is nevertheless evident enough, since there must be a sufficient cause to account for the fact that it is he, Sākyamuni, and not some other man, who discovered the way out of the karmic wheel of births and deaths, or rather that particular way which is specifically Buddha-given and which alone is in question here; it is he alone who 'has broken his existence like a breastplate'. This uniqueness of funtion or miracle, which at first effaces itself before the Law because it is not its specific contents, had to be affirmed in its turn according to its own nature and in its quality of divine gift; this happened, firstly under the form of the monastic initiation instituted by the Buddha and secondly through the later sermons: initiatic power, on any showing, presupposes a 'divine nature' and, as for the later sermons, it should be remembered that some of these Scriptures belong not only to the Mahāyāna but also to Theravāda Buddhism. These sermons are noticeably different from those embodying the Law; they reveal the metaphysics of the Void, which will subsequently take on a doctrinal aspect with Nagārjuna and a purely 'experimental' aspect with the school of Dhyāna or Zen whereof Boddhidharma was the great initiator; the 'Flower Sermon', with its silent gesture, is evidently independent of any written formulation. Yet another expression of the personal reality of the Buddha is the saving invocation of the name of Amitābha and lastly the sacramental image of the Tathāgata, 'Him thus come', as mentioned above, that true 'manifestation of the Void" (*shūnyamūrti*) and 'expression of the Inexpressible'. All these aforementioned elements derive from the aspect that here has been called the 'being' of the Buddha by way of distinguishing it from his general and more or less externalized teaching.

*

The 'Great Vehicle' (*Mahāyāna*) possesses a mysterious dimension known as the 'Adamantine Vehicle' or Vajrayāna. In order to gain an insight into what this means, one has to start out from the idea of the 'metaphysical transparency of the world'; that is to say one has to base oneself on a perspective according to which (to quote an expression of Pascal's) Reality is 'an infinite sphere whose centre is everywhere and its circumference nowhere': it is this circumference and this centre which are represented, in the adamantine doctrine, by the Buddha Mahāvairōchana ('the Great Illuminator') who is at one and the same time (if we may use Vedantine terms here) *Atmā*, *Īshvara* and *Buddhi*, that is to say Supra-ontological Essence, Ontological Essence and Universal Intellect. This metaphysical transparency everywhere refers effect back to cause without, however, doing away with the irreversible nature of the causal relationship at the level of the world; the Absolute is in no wise causal in itself, since in reality nothing can be outside It, but it is causal when considered from the point of view of the Cosmos which, for its part, is real in virtue of the metaphysical reduction of effect to cause and in no other sense. Thus 'all is *Ātmā*, Self' or 'all is *Shūnya*, Void' or 'Vairōchana' or 'solarity' if we pay heed to the etymology as well as the symbolism of this Sanskrit name; but nothing in itself, *qua* existential 'accident', is the Self or the Void or the solar Buddha.

To illustrate the structure of this metaphysical vision of things recourse can be had to the following symbol: the spider's web, formed of warp and weft threads or of radii and concentric circles, represents the Universe under the twofold relationship of essential identity and existential separation; the synthesis of these two relationships will be indicated by the spiral. From the point of view of the radii a given thing *is* the Principle, represented in this scheme by the central point; from the point of view of the concentric circles, a given thing only *represents* that Principle; from the point of view of the spiral, however, it can be said that such and such a thing is an *emanation* or *manifestation*, therefore that it is neither the Principle as such nor simply an image of It. In a general way it can be said that the West – European philosophy and Semitic exotericism – is attached chiefly to the second relationship, that of existential discontinuity or separation, of concentric circles and of more or less 'proximity' to the Centre, whereas the East – Semitic esotericism and Asian metaphysics generally – will prefer the first named relationship, that of radii and identity of essence, therefore also of the metaphysical transparency of all things.

It is an inevitable error attaching to an exoteric view of things that one is practically compelled thereby to opt for a 'lesser truth', for the sake of avoiding a greater evil, in the form of believing that 'Creation' is an absolutely closed and quasi-autonomous system; in other words, one finds oneself compelled to believe in an 'absolute creation' in the same way as one believes in an absolute God: the error resides in this parallelism. In truth, God is absolutely Himself, but the world is only world in a relative sense; if on the one hand one can sometimes speak of a thing as being 'relatively absolute' one could never, on the other hand, describe anything as 'absolutely relative'. It is true to say that Creation *as such* is entirely created (or manifested), but precisely these words 'as such' neither cover all its nature nor entirely explain its possibility. But to return to the spider and its symbolism: this, with the solar form of its web, calls forth a vision of Being – or the Self – drawing forth the Cosmos from itself and 'eating' the beings to be found within the latter; 'deification', for man, is to be assimilated by God.

The great truth, or the great experience represented by the Vajrayāna is to show how each thing, each focus of energy, by the very fact that it exists and that, existing, it is something of *That* which makes it to exist, constitutes a possible entry towards the Real and towards Deliverance; universal Buddha-hood implies the fact that each consciousness, being Buddha essentially, can become 'That which it is'. Granted the description of esotericism as a short cut not within reach of every mental make-up or every degree of intellectual scope, the Adamantine Vehicle, with its perspective of 'ubiquity' and its quasi-theurgic instrument of *mantra* – the invocation of a holy Name or sentence – provides a most significant illustration of what an esoteric method consists of, both theoretically, in the realm of vision, and operatively, in the realm of realization.

In the same connection it is worth recalling here a highly suggestive comparison once made to the author by a Japanese Buddhist: the sound of Christian bells, so he was saying, draws man upward and leads him beyond the world; but the heavy and deep sound of the Buddhist bell leaves us motionless, it makes us come down into ourselves, into our supra-personal Centre. Here is an instructive confrontation of two spiritual perspectives which, however, has nothing irreducible about it: on the one side there is 'dynamic elevation' and sublimation of becoming, while on the other there is 'static profundity' and repose in one's essential being.

CHAPTER III

CHARITY AND EXISTENCE

Pity or Charity, or rather a particular manner of stressing this quality, is one of the features wherein Buddhism and Christianity resemble one another. It is, however, important to avoid confusing this charity with a vague and flabby attitude; in other words, charity is not a sentimentalism that causes one to be blind to the objective differences of phenomena, nor is it equatable with a 'psychologism' that reduces all culpability to nothing. It is one thing not to tell a wolf from a lamb and quite another to recognize their distinction on the plane of contingencies even while perceiving the ontological coincidence of opposites and remaining uninvolved in the dead end of passional illusion and in the gearing of concordant action and reaction, *karma*. As in the case of Christ's Law requiring one to love one's enemy and turn the other cheek, so also for a Buddhist this is essentially a case of getting beyond the plane of affective contrasts and this, in view of a reality, or of the Reality, which contains all things and is situated beyond all things; a Christian would say 'for love of God'. It is a pernicious error to suppose that serenity of soul is blind and levelling; on the contrary, its only value is in virtue of its own lucidity: 'resist not evil' only makes sense on condition that we remain aware that on a certain plane that concerns us unquestionably as living beings the bad is other than the good. There are few things as stifling as the sentimentalist's attempt 'to see only the good everywhere' or 'only to see evil in oneself' at the expense of Truth and in disregard of human balance; for just as generosity only has value if one is strong, so does the perception of unity only make sense for one who is capable of discerning diversity.

Charity, in the sense intended here, is to try and discover in those whom we have to judge the qualities they really possess, and not to attribute to them blindly qualities to which they are strangers or which in no wise counterbalance their defects. The value of charity, in fact, depends on its contents; outside truth, charity is nothing. It is an outrage on intelligence to forego our power of judgment for the sole pleasure of persuading ourselves that we are charitable; it is true that such a proceeding may sometimes have a certain ascetic meaning, circumstances permitting, but neither is it, in that case, devoid of a certain selfishness.

And the following is important: an external attitude, whatever may be its usefulness, always remains an approximation, not a totality; it has the value of a symbol or a key, not that of a rigorous adequation, otherwise hypocrisy would not be a possibility: no more than in the case of Scriptural symbolism have moral exteriorizations to be taken literally, for here as elsewhere 'the letter killeth, but the spirit giveth life'. Buddhist charity is above all a spiritual view of things, it is therefore transcendent in relation to its own possible forms: one proof of this is the fact that Buddhists, despite their basic objection to taking life, have not automatically adopted the idea of abolishing the death penalty; in this respect they differ much from the contemporary 'psychologism' which so readily forgets both the charity owing to society and also, in a final analysis, the charity appertaining to the condemned person himself, of which a due exercise may not always preclude a relatively painful solution and this, for reasons that are by no means confined to the social interest. It is worth noting, in this connection, that in an ardently Buddhist country like Tibet, where the population is numerically small and criminality comparatively sparse, there has been a tendency, much accentuated in recent times, to substitute other severe punishments for the death penalty; a similar attitude has been observable among another mountain people, the Hunzas, who after all are Muslims and therefore traditionally less committed than their Buddhist neighbours to a general objection against taking life.

Certainly, Buddhism is averse to all forms of violence; but from a Buddhist standpoint the only firm conclusion to be drawn from this fact is that perfection is only possible in the framework of monastic renunciation;[1] life in the world doubtless comprises unavoidable or necessary evils, but this is because 'the world' is an evil in itself. Strictly speaking, there is no good to be found outside the Three Refuges – the Buddha, the Law and the Community.

Particular questions of application apart, let it especially be remembered that if the Tathāgata be free from all vice, as assuredly he is, he stands equally above all the virtues as far as these will consist of distinctive properties and are associated with an illusory consciousness: a devilish counterfeit of this wisdom would be to declare oneself independent of virtues one does not possess. It is against this general background that Charity, like everything else, has to be assessed.

To love all beings without distinction is to love that Being which is to be found in all things alike, it is therefore to love the Divine or the Void whence every creature springs and it is to love, in the creature, the centre where it ceases to be itself or where there is nothing else to be found but Selfhood, no virtue, no vice, nor any other determination whatsoever. Nevertheless it is proper to distinguish clearly between a unitive vision that includes all beings as the outcome of a spiritual realization and a mental attitude that tries to anticipate this realization by resorting to sentimentalities and mirages deriving from egocentric motives of any kind.

While we are on the subject and by way of a spiritual parallel, it will not be inopportune to sum-up briefly the monotheistic doctrine concerning human charity; this special reference would be superfluous were it not for a certain terminology associated with the Semitic religions whereby the teaching in question, though of quite universal applicability, has become blurred in the consciousness of many people, being replaced there by social concepts having no connection with

[1] Here the word 'monastic' must be given, not only its normal connotation of membership of the Sangha (instituted by the Buddha to provide just such a framework), but also of any comparable spiritual attitude regardless of the nature of its formal structure; it denotes 'poverty in spirit' in the widest sense. The word *faqir* (= 'poor man') in Islam denotes a selfsame attitude; for such a man the whole world is his hermitage or his monastery.

traditional truth; in fact, this kind of confusion occurs every-where, in the East as well as in the West.

That which counts in the sight of the Absolute and in relation to our last ends is a charity formed in virtue of the 'love of God' and accepted for the sake of that same love; apart from this, human life has no meaning either for him who gives or for him who receives. The same holds good for work: far from con-stituting a merit in itself work only becomes meritorious on condition it is carried out for love of God; which in its turn implies that the work be done as well as possible and that its contents, as 'work of art', are such as to transmit something of the truth, of spirit, of that which gives meaning to life. It can, however, happen sometimes that charity is exercised out of love of God but on behalf of someone who fails to profit from it in view of God; or again it may happen that someone exercises charity without loving God but on behalf of another who does profit from it spiritually: in both these cases the gain is one-sided, while the other party will only have served as an instrument of destiny, *karma* in human form. Is it to be inferred from this that charity should only be practised towards those who are supposed to profit thereby in view of their last ends? If such an alternative is clearly offered, yes; otherwise not. But even in a case where choice is possible, one will still practise charity towards an 'unbeliever' when it seems that this might somehow help to cure his soul and on condition that the needy 'believer' is not thereby harmed in respect of a vital interest; the same holds good when the need of the 'unbeliever' is of a more important order than that of the believer and when this supposed act of charity is not harmful in an ultimate sense to those who do it.

One additional point to be noted is this: poverty, no more than illness or any other sad happening in life, does not carry with it in the sight of God any 'right' to impiety, displeasing as this may sound to those religious demagogues who, under pressure of a materialistic and atheistic environment, bow before this kind of blackmail. Love of the Divine is a categorical imperative which, coming from Heaven, cannot fail to take account of the limits of our nature or of our human responsi-bility and which, consequently, could not depend *de jure* on any social or economic condition whatsoever. The requirement for us to recognize the Absolute is itself an absolute one, it concerns man as such and not man under such and such conditions. It is a fundamental aspect of human dignity, and especially of that intelligence which denotes 'the state of man hard to obtain', that we accept Truth because it is true and for no other reason.

CHAPTER IV

THE QUESTION OF ILLUSION

THE idea of Universal illusion or the unreality of the world, *Māyā*, constitutes something like an insurmountable barrier between the Western 'personalism' and the Oriental metaphysics: Hindus are reproached for denying the world or else for identifying the world with God, and Buddhists are likewise blamed for denying the soul – as if Nirvāna were not the prototype of the soul and its summit – and in so doing the would-be critics do not ask themselves what part is played in all this by terminological contingencies; for only too often it happens that discussion begins about attributes before there has been agreement about things in themselves. Buddhists deny 'the soul', so it is said, and yet they admit both essentially and in practice the 'karmic' continuity or, if one so prefers, the moral causality of that living and conscious nucleus that is the human *ego*.

Individuation takes place in proportion as the movement of the cosmic wheel is rapid: just as water when shaken becomes dispersed in innumerable drops, so likewise the Self becomes segmented, in illusory mode and without thereby being affected in its immutability, in innumerable particular subjects: the current of forms becomes the torrent of souls. The current of forms is at one and the same time movement and division; where the rotation of the cosmic wheel takes place, there also occurs the dispersal of souls, individuation with its numberless modalities; the *ego* is a quasi-physical consequence of this universal rotation. On the other hand, where there is calm, there also access can be gained to the immutable and indivisible Selfhood; where the centre is, there Unity is to be found. And just as the cosmic wheel is 'none other' than the Self, on pain of

34

non-existence, so also Selfhood can arise everywhere as a miracle of salvation.

The very absurdity of a plurality of *egos* shows that here there can but be question of an optical illusion on the macrocosmic scale, of an existential unbalance which, as such, cannot continue indefinitely; each ego presents itself as a flagrant contradiction, a 'scandal' that reason comes up against just as it does against the 'finite infinity' of time and space. The empirical 'I' is nothing but a shifting tissue of images or tendencies – the *Milinda Panha* admirably illustrates this theme, which runs through the whole of Buddhism: when the *ego* of a certain individual eight years old is compared with the *ego* of the same individual at eighty years of age one may well ask oneself where is the real I? And if a man could live on for a thousand years, what would be left of that which was his 'I' in the first century of his life? Beings and events would drift around him like leaves scattered by the wind, even the sky would end by becoming a crushing burden, his body would be like a coffin – unless indeed the man were to surmount his *ego* in such wise as to perceive the face of God in all things like a new sky whose infinity both stabilizes and liberates; but then even this world would no longer be 'of this world' for that man, it would have become a kind of beyond.

Man gets attached to his scanty memories because he in practice confuses these with his own self, as if there were not to be found outside him, before him, after him, impressions, destinies, memories fairer and richer than his own and to which he will never have access. He clings to his reminiscences as if a mental image, whatever may be its value, could ever be identified with one's immortal personality. Man is incapable of viewing an object from all sides at once or under all its aspects – it is impossible for him to enjoy at the same time every aspect of a precious thing or of a beloved being; in the carnal ecstasy, a creature can no longer enjoy any visual perception of form and this is an impoverishment of a kind even while at the same time foreshadowing the extinction of the soul in God. Bliss is only possible beyond all those formal crystallizations to which passion clings; that is why in earthly pleasure one thing precludes another, all is measured out in space and time and one happiness always implies forgetfulness, if one may so put it, of a thousand other possible happinesses.

The foregoing considerations bring us close to the Buddhist (and the Vedantine) idea of the unreality of the world; in order to render this idea more familiar, a certain imaginative power can be called into play by putting the vital question in an inverse sense: what then is the meaning of the common assumption that the world is real, absolutely real? How can one apply the label 'real', without conveying the slightest attenuation of meaning, to phenomena which become seemingly reduced to nothing, not indeed in their immediate and momentary surroundings, but as soon as they are considered in relation to space and time in all their indefinite extension? No one denies the relative reality of such and such a tree, such a fleck of foam, such a dream; but what does that tree represent on the scale of the galaxies and what does its brief life mean, even if it lasts for centuries, in relation to geological periods reducible, as these are, to mere instants in their turn? What is the reality of a tiny drop of water beside the ocean and its ages-long existence? People will doubtless reply that all the world knows after a fashion that time is relative, but this is not the question, for there is knowing and knowing: who then is the man who 'lives' in a concrete sense both the simultaneity and the evanescence of things to the point of being able to rise above himself and by that very fact to grasp the dreamlike character of the current of forms? But there is also ignorance on the plane of things that are naturally simultaneous, that is to say there is the inability of most men to 'be' the others, to live two lives or all lives at once, so to speak: if man feels so much at ease within his own narrow limits, this is because his imagination does not enable him to be conscious of what is happening to such other people, on other continents, in other spiritual worlds. In practice, a want of imagination is, for many people, a condition of happiness, since it helps to confer that easy assurance which most men need in order to feel happy, failing a happiness of a superior order gained on the ruins of a previous equilibrium; it might almost be said that man requires errors in order to be able to sleep at ease: in that sense 'ignorance is bliss' for the many, hence their instinctive reluctance to be awakened. The whole drama of worldliness and Buddhahood is there.

The Divine Intellect, free as it is of all infirmity, knows things both in their succession and in their simultaneity; it beholds the logical unfolding of things as well as their global possibility; knowing all substances, it knows at one and the same time all their 'accidents' at the level of reality – or of unreality – that belongs to them respectively. Such and such a man in the Middle Ages is walking in such and such a town and thinks he is living 'now', in which supposition he is not more deceived than ourselves of course; now if that man while crossing his own street, thinks deeply of the Real, of God, he will immediately shed that aspect of temporal and spacial illusion that separated him from us here; the street, in its false actuality, will limit him no longer, he will have come out of the deceptive instantaneity of his bodily situation, whether spacially or psychologically considered; while thinking of God he is at our side, and not only that: he is everywhere, at the side of all beings, in all worlds; he is, in a sense, wherever the Absolute has ever been thought of or will be thought of, he is like an eyewitness of everything whatsoever.

When we speak of the Absolute here, this could refer to an Absolute still relative in itself, to make use of a somewhat paradoxical expression; but this 'relatively absolute', creative and saving principle of Being remains in fact absolute in relation to man as such; its relativity only applies *in divinis* and in the Intellect. In the picture previously given, any question of unconsciousness in the subject or of his lack of imagination no longer counts, for it is as if he were endowed with a consciousness of all things at once from the very moment that his mind is directed on the divine Void and that, by so doing or rather by so being, he becomes situated at the centre of space and time.

But there is not only the question of the unreality of the Cosmos to be reckoned with; there is also the question of its relative reality, therefore of the identity of essence – a mysterious and almost ineffable identity – between manifestation and the Principle or between symbols and their Prototype or in other words between Samsāra and Nirvāna. In *such and such* a light or *such and such* an intelligence we are meeting Light or Intelligence *as such*, therefore all the light and intelligence that is: this word 'such' firstly expresses a particularity or accidentality and after that, in the expression 'as such', it expresses essence or reality, the divine Suchness. That which is not identical is different, that which is not different is identical; the world, whether as macrocosm or human microcosm, is 'neither divine nor non-divine', or else it possesses both these qualities at once. Formulations of this kind, apparently simplified to the point of unreason (as commonly happens with antinomian expressions), demand more than simple logic for their understanding, for they call into play that which, in the intelligence, is most mysterious according to the saying 'He (God) set his eye upon their hearts, that he might show them the greatness of his works'(*Ecclesiasticus* XVII, 8).

CHAPTER V

A BUDDHIST EYE ON SCIENCE

For Buddhism, as for Vedānta, every kind of error, all sin even, is ultimately reducible to the error of 'false attribution', that is to say to a reading of absoluteness into what is relative and, consequently also, of relativity into the absolute. The most typical expression of this error consists in treating the empirical 'I' as 'self'; the specifically Buddhist doctrine of *anātmā*, 'non-selfhood', so often misunderstood by Western inquirers, is expressly aimed at this kind of confusion.

In view of what has already been said on the subject of the Cosmic Illusion and its various implications it would seem desirable to dwell somewhat longer on this question and draw attention to the part played by the common illusion concerning the possibility of an 'absolutely real' in relativity. Many of the philosophical sophistries prevalent in the contemporary world derive from this cause; in particular, it is from here that has sprung an empirical and experimental science claiming to unveil the metaphysical mystery of Existence itself by such palpably relative means as giant telescopes or electronic microscopes, for instance[1].

Those who seek to enclose the Universe in their shortsighted logic fail to take stock, at least in practice, of the fact that the sum of possible phenomenal knowledge is *per se* inexhaustible and that, consequently, the sum of our present 'scientific' information represents a nothing beside our ignorances – in short that 'there are more things in heaven and earth than are dreamt of in your philosophy'. They fail to see that, in order to

[1] Goethe, when he refused to look through a microscope because he did not wish to wrench from Nature what she is unwilling to offer to our human senses, displayed a most just intuition of the limits circumscribing all natural science, and at the same time of the limits of the human sphere itself.

extend our means of investigation to fit the scale of the total cosmos, we would have to start off by multiplying the human senses in mathematical progression, which in fact brings us back to the unlimited, therefore also to the inaccessible and the unknowable. In all this wish to accumulate knowledge of relative things the metaphysical dimension, which alone takes us out of the vicious circle of the phenomenal and the absurd, is expressly shelved; it is as if a man were to be endowed with all possible faculties of perception minus intelligence; or again, it is as if one believed that an animal endowed with sight was more capable than a blind man of understanding the mysteries of the world.

The science of our time knows how to measure galaxies and split atoms, but it is incapable of the smallest investigation beyond the sensible world, so much so that outside its own self-imposed but unrecognized limits it remains more ignorant than the most rudimentary magic. It will doubtless be objected that modern psychology, for its part, is not a science riveted to matter, but this plea fails to take note of the exclusively empirical character of that science: it remains a system of observations and hypotheses, already compromised in advance by the fact that those who practise it are ignorant of the profounder nature of the phenomena they set out to study. A science, to merit that name truly, owes us an explanation of a determinate order of phenomena; now modern science, which claims to be all-embracing by the very fact that it recognizes nothing outside itself as valid, is quite unable to explain to us, for instance, what a sacred book really amounts to or what is a saint or a miracle; it knows nothing of God or of the beyond or of the Intellect and it cannot even tell us anything about premonition and telepathy though both of these evidently belong to the phenomenal order; it does not know in virtue of what principle or possibility Shamanistic procedures may cure illnesses or attract rain. All attempts at explanations regarding things of this order, let alone those of a spiritual order, are vitiated basically through a defect of imagination: all things are viewed in function, firstly of empirical 'matter' (even if called by some other name) and, secondly, of the evolutionary hypothesis, instead of primary consideration being given to the principial emanation of 'ideas' and the progressive coagulation of substances, in conformity with the principle of individuation on the one hand and of 'demiurgic solidification' on the other. Where the *Perennial Philosophy* says 'Principle, emanation, substance' modern science will say 'energy, matter, evolution'. As far as emanation is concerned, it is necessary to stress its principial and discontinuous character: emanation does not take away anything from the Principle: the world is not *a part* of God.

The trouble is that people try to explain 'horizontally', at the surface of things, that which is only explainable in a 'vertical' sense, in depth; it is as if we were living in a glacial world where water was unknown and where only the Revelations mentioned it, whereas profane science in that case would persist in denying its existence. Such a science is assuredly cut to the measure of modern man who conceived it in the first place and who is at the same time its product; like him, that science by implication claims a sort of immunity, one might even say an 'extra-territoriality', in the face of the Absolute; like him, his science keeps itself apart from any cosmic or eschatological context.

To all the above considerations the following may also be added: science, like the machine, has reversed the respective roles, turning its creators into its own creatures; it escapes from the control of intelligence as such from the moment that it claims to define the nature of intelligence from the outside and from below. Our timeless cosmic environment was deprived of its function of teaching us a great truth when it became replaced by a 'stage setting': the stellar vault has been turned into the extension of a laboratory, bodily beauty is reduced to a mechanism of natural selection and no more. People no longer sense the fact that the quantitative richness of a knowledge – of any kind of knowledge – necessarily entails an interior impoverishment unless accompanied by a spiritual science able to maintain balance and re-establish unity. The common man, if he were able to travel through interplanetary space, would come back to earth terribly impoverished, even if his reason had not meanwhile collapsed from sheer horror. This picture brings us back to the forbidden tree of Genesis of which the drama goes on repeating itself at wide intervals down to our own times; 'decentralized' man whose mind is surfeited with discontinuous facts is prey to a hopeless poverty and this moreover explains those nihilistic and anguished philosophies current in our time. The ancients doubtless did not know how to prolong lives which nevertheless had a meaning; the moderns know how to prolong lives that are becoming increasingly meaningless; moreover the ancients by the very fact that they saw a meaning in life, also saw one in death.

If life be but a faint glow between two nights or two nothings and if we be only products of a biological hazard devoid of interest in an absurd universe, what then is the use of all these efforts and, more especially, what is the use of a scientific faith even more absurd than the senseless universe that men ceaselessly explore without ever a hope of coming out of it? And of what profit to us are accurate observations if in practice – for in principle they are innocent – they deprive us of all that is essential, namely the knowledge of that whereof natural phenomena are but fragile exteriorisations? Far from being unknowable in themselves, these higher realities can be perceived through these same phenomena inasmuch as they become metaphysically transparent to the truly observant eye; but these realities also reveal themselves through the great prophetic, messianic and avatāric manifestations which address themselves *a priori* to the recipient human collectivities in order to communicate to them truths which, in fact, they have become incapable of apprehending directly.

To avoid all misunderstanding it must be stressed here that no branch of science is evil because of its contents; but a demonstration of anatomy, possibly very useful to an adult, might yet ruin a child's soul. To discern the realities which phenomena at once veil and reveal is part of spiritual science, to which the natural sciences, when not abused, offer no logical contradiction. It is, however, necessary to be warned that the perspective relating to the metaphysical transparency of phenomena, if not kept in just balance, can harden into an attitude that is the parent of a real idolatry; between the symbolical penetration of phenomena and their virtual divinisation there are many stages, some harmless and others dangerous as the case may be. When idolatry has become a collective attitude, the only way out is through a theology of apparently abstract character.

God, inasmuch as He is Intelligence, subsists as the 'absolute subconscious' of all beings; this word is here used provisionally and in a purely extrinsic sense in order to denote a functional analogy as seen 'from the outside'; since it is evident that by rights it is of 'supra-consciousness' one should be speaking here. The divine Self is infinite Knowledge, whereas the sub-conscious of the psychologists can be anything you please. As used by them, the subconscious covers all whereof we have had no consciousness in an actual sense, be it a matter of higher realities or of psychic complexes; but in practice, people under-stand by the word 'subconscious' merely the inferior psychism, as is moreover consistent with its etymology wherever *sub* is opposed to *super* or *supra*. If the word 'infra-conscious' were a current term, this should serve to indicate, not that of which we ourselves are but faintly conscious, but rather that which is endowed with only a faint degree of consciousness.

Just as the ordinary subconscious of any man, given that it is actualized thanks to some cause or other, is able to reveal things not perceived in space and time, so also this 'absolute Subconscious' reveals to men, across the divinely inspired Messages or through the Intellect as the case may be, that of which they stand in need and even infinitely in need. This possibility of actualizing the 'Universal Subconscious' is conferred by the very nature of the human species; the immense importance accorded by Buddhism, and by other religions in their own way, to 'human birth hard to obtain' is bound up with this possibility of Enlightenment, whether indirectly and by stages or else directly, as in a flash: the mystery of awakening into Buddhahood is all there. In the light of this supreme characteristic of mankind it can be declared that the very existence of religions proves both the Absolute and immortality, although this is but a manner of speaking, since a 'proof' of the Absolute can only amount to an indication: that is to say, a metaphysical argument will at best serve to call forth an intellection or to actualize a pre-existing and immanent reminiscence; which amounts to saying that one cannot prove the Absolute outside Itself and also that one cannot prove the existence of light to blind men.

Modern science cheerfully rejects the traditional wisdoms without taking account of the fact that this rejection comes up against an improbable disproportion between the intelligence of believers *qua* men and the hypothetical absurdity of their beliefs, as also against the no less impossible disproportion between the intelligence of the Sages and the supposed absurdity of their convictions and their intimate motives. Man is intelligence before all else, therefore he also is wisdom and contemplation and, by further consequence, he is tradition; to detach man from the latter, far from rendering him independent, is to deprive him of his human quality.

In a similar order of ideas, what answer should be given to the following question: why did Providence leave man in ignorance of certain things, on the plane of the sensible world, which he was bound to discover in the long run? Given that prevention is better than cure and that Heaven could not but foresee the disastrous repercussions, materially and psychologically, of the modern discoveries and inventions, it had every interest (so one might argue) in speaking to man about palaeontology and molecular physics and in 'situating' these things in relation to the Absolute and immortality. Perhaps the best answer to this kind of question is that Revelation, always preoccupied with 'the one thing needful' and conscious, as it must be, of the uselessness and harmfulness of a purely external and quantitative form of knowledge, had no call to set the example of that which it wished to avoid or the coming of which it wished at least to delay.

There is, however, yet another reason to be considered, one that is doubtless less fundamental but nonetheless convincing from the point of view of the present discussion: it was indeed necessary – since 'there must needs be scandal' – that the men of the 'latter times' should find in their own surroundings occasions for believing themselves superior to their ancestors and too clever to accept Revelation; consequently it was necessary to reserve a possible form of knowledge, one that (consequences notwithstanding) is in itself spiritually indifferent, for the purpose of corroborating and feeding the illusions of the Age of Darkness, the age when the Law of the Buddha shall be forgotten, that Law which in the beginning was 'lived' and in subsequent stages of the cosmic cycle was merely 'imitated' in diminishing degree: the next chapter will have something more to say about this question of cyclic development, particularly important for an understanding of the Indian traditions. All this can be summed up, implicitly, in the well-known saying of the Buddha: 'And why have I taught you nothing about the world? Because this would be of no use to you for obtaining the knowledge of the causes of suffering, for the ceasing of suffering, for Nirvāna'.

Buddhism provides a decisive argument against any science purporting to be an end in itself and therefore also, by anticipation and in principle, against the contemporary Western scientism; the pith of its argument, which is of universal applicability, consists in the undeniable fact that by becoming 'objectively' preoccupied with the phenomenal world man inevitably becomes drawn into the morass of conjectures and illusions and therefore drawn away from the possibility of Deliverance. The wish for exactitude professed by this science is far from constituting a guarantee of intrinsic value and spiritual legitimacy, for the simple reason that the 'exactitude' in question is already jeopardized by the most monstrous possible begging of the question: scientism, by denying the Intellect and the Absolute, rejects *a priori* the criterion and measure of all knowledge. 'They do not understand that the objective world derives from Mind itself' says the *Lankāvatāra-Sūtra*, 'and do not grasp that the whole system of thought likewise derives from Mind; but attributing reality to these manifestations of Mind they examine them, senseless people that they are, and get attached to dualities such as "this and that" or "being and not being", without perceiving that there is but a single Essence'.

CHAPTER VI

COSMOLOGICAL AND ESCHATOLOGICAL VIEWPOINTS

THE consideration of world cycles is a common feature of Hindu and Buddhist cosmology, though the two traditions display important differences as to detail. In Buddhism the *kalpas*, *manvantaras* and *mahāyugas* of the Hindus are replaced by *mahākalpas*, *asankhyeyas* and *antarakalpas*, that is to say by quite different cyclic divisions indicating periods of quasi-incalculable duration. The Buddhist, as compared with the Hindu, conceptions seem to be determined by a perspective that is in some senses a dynamic one; it is as if one were comparing a moving spiral with a system of static factors such as squares and triangles. This subject is mentioned here, however, not so much for the sake of listing analogies and divergences between two traditional forms as because it provides an opportunity to develop a few considerations of principle regarding the various eschatologies and their profound concordances. If religious doctrines about the Universe and the beyond differ much among themselves, this is due on the one hand to the diversity of viewpoints and aspects, therefore also of subjective as well as objective positions and, on the other, because here one is treating of a realm that is *per se* impossible to describe in human language. In a certain sense, each religion is in the right versus the others, failing which any exoteric presentation of religion would be nothing but a snare; but in fact, an exotericism is by definition unable of itself to take cognizance of the relationship whereby, at one and the same time, it is justified in its claims yet limited in scope: the total Truth remains nonetheless one in its limitless and transcendent validity.

The macrocosm – the assemblage of worlds and cosmic cycles – is an inexhaustible realm, consonantly with the indeterminate nature of Universal Substance; as such, it cannot therefore become the object of any scientific investigation claiming to lead to a polyvalent and definitive result. Otherwise put, the macrocosm is neither our visible world nor is it God: it is possible for us to know creation and the Creator, or the 'I' and the 'Self' – with all the reservations and conditions that impose themselves as the case may demand – but it is not possible for us to know the totality of the phenomena of the Universe: the latter escapes perception whether by the thinking mind, which is especially made for knowing our world, or by the Intellect, which is especially made for knowing the Absolute. Consequently, man has to be content with fragmentary visions or symbolic syntheses and with elliptical formulations which will never satisfy his curiosity entirely and which it would be idle to try and complete by means of logical operations necessarily pre-condemned to frustration: for, let it be said once again, the indefinitely diverse or inconceivably complex is not the normal and ultimate content of human intelligence. Muslims express an analogous idea when they say that the seat of the Devil is situated – subjectively speaking, not factually – between man and God, that is to say in the imagination which, like Samsāra, is for ever shifting and indefinite. In reality, many of the contradictions to be found in sacred texts only serve to circumscribe indirectly things that are in fact indescribable; if Heaven does not hesitate sometimes to use language that sounds absurd, this is because a seeming absurdity, which is unavoidable in the case we are considering, is yet able to communicate fragmentary but nonetheless indispensable indications concerning the interconnection of worlds and cycles, and even much more than this.

Howbeit, it is certainly not going too far, in this sphere of things and even while adhering to very schematic viewpoints, to remark that the various traditional notions of cosmology and eschatology – creation or manifestation, deluge, last judgment, resurrection of the body, renewal of the world, heavens and hells, transmigration, cosmic days and nights etc. – refer to universal rhythms or, if one may so put it, to the 'breathing of the Self', together with all the primary and secondary phases of affirmation and negation, exteriorization and introversion, projection and reintegration that these rhythms comprise. The origin as also the end of the world, of matter, of life, are already hard enough to express in the symbolically suggestive language of traditional doctrine; they are beyond the reach, *a fortiori* and in an absolute sense, of the investigations of a science that is purely rational and experimental. One of the chief fallacies of such a science is precisely this, namely that it implicitly lends to matter (however it may understand this term) a fixed character as of an invariable basis, whereas physical substance (in its actual and 'post-edenic' state) really is only a kind of 'accidental' crystallization of the subtle substance (the *sūkshma sharīra* of the Hindus); whatever may be its own consistency or its quality it is none other than the extreme limit or 'point of precipitation' (for our sensible world) of the demiurgic process of manifestation. The Universe is a tissue of worlds and cycles; outside our human cosmos space and time stop, or rather they are replaced by other conditions of existence – analogous conditions doubtless (Existence being one) but unimaginable for us. Some will perhaps raise an objection here by saying that modern physics is perfectly prepared to admit the variability and evolution of matter-energy, or rather, that it has abandoned the childish notion of 'matter', which it has replaced by 'movement' or by the ternary idea of 'mass-space-time'; but this really does not affect the argument since this same physics neither allows the non-material nor the supra-sensible to enter into its calculations.

The human microcosm is like a circle the centre of which is situated on the circumference of a larger circle, namely the sensible macrocosm, and the centre of this second circle in its turn is situated on a still larger circumference, representing the total Macrocosm. A cosmos or a cycle essentially is something that *becomes* and that ceases to be; Buddhism provides the clearest vision of this principle. For man, there are three *cosmoi* or cycles to consider, firstly the soul, secondly the world which is the soul's medium of manifestation and lastly the Universe of which that world represents but a minute fragment. The difference between the 'particular judgment' and the 'Last Judgment', or between death and the end of the world, consists herein, namely that at the time of death only the soul (and not the body, which belongs strictly to our own world) is reabsorbed in the direction of the Principle in order to be 'judged' (in terms of its individual *karma*, as Buddhists would say), whereas at the time of this world's ending it is the latter that is thus absorbed. But there is yet a third and ultimate reabsorption to be reckoned with, the one marking the end of all manifestation: for 'the chosen' this is not an ending but an 'exaltation' in the Uncreated Light. In Hindu parlance, this is the *mahāpralaya*, the great return into undifferentiation (*pralaya* being this return when applied to our world only) and doubtless such is also the meaning of the *apokatastasis* of Western Antiquity and of certain Gnostics.

Concerning the remembrance of 'all their past lives' common to all Buddhas it is important not to lose sight of the fact that the Buddha possesses or comprises all possible destinies; furthermore, it must not be forgotten when considering the innumerable 'incarnations' of one and the same soul – or to be more precise, of one and the same 'karmic nexus' – that the chances of attaining Deliverance are very slight in the majority of states to be traversed; the Christian concept of '*limbo*' and of the regimen of the dead anterior to Christ's coming and outside Christ's fold is like a symbolical expression of the same idea.

In order to understand the differences of doctrinal language distinguishing the various traditions from one another it is necessary to take account of the following: a perspective which is focussed on the Absolute and which because of this very fact belongs to pure intellectual contemplation will tend to stress the relativity of the cosmos; hence doctrines like that of transmigration. On the other hand, a perspective that considers the Absolute in relation to man and that 'humanizes' It in consequence (in which case it will be a question, not of the purely Absolute, but of Being) will readily lend an absolute character to certain relativities; relativities doubtless marked by the Absolute, but of a cosmic order nonetheless. Buddhism and Christianity respectively represent these two perspectives, whence the difference of their symbolical language and mode of expression generally. Moreover, by a paradoxical compensation, the immediately metaphysical perspective will seem to efface the 'hiatus' between the Absolute and the relative, whereas it is the cosmological and religious perspective that will, on the contrary, seem to maintain the purity and transcendence of the Divine, even while giving it a relative slant and even while affirming the 'compact reality' of the cosmos.

From a monotheistic and Western point of view it may seem strange that Buddhism, as also Hinduism, only takes very scant account of the possibility of obtaining what the Confucio-Taoist tradition calls the state of 'longevity'. The explanation lies in the fact that the first named perspectives, being metaphysically and not 'humanistically' orientated, envisage Deliverance outside any and every world; they therefore start out from the alternative 'Existence-Deliverance' and not, as in the case of the Judeo-European view of things, from the alternative 'damnation-salvation'. In other words, the Far-Eastern and Indian perspectives have no presumptive interest in individualistic solutions; they do not wish to compromise Deliverance by lingering over solutions that still appertain to the realm of *Māyā* although, in a secondary way they do in fact admit such solutions, two cases in point being the Vishnuite forms of Hinduism and in Buddhism the Pure Land doctrine on its more exoteric side (for the other side exists there too, under cover of the same symbolism, otherwise one could hardly speak here of an integrally Buddhist tradition which this certainly is): however, in the present context it is on the general and determining form of the doctrine that stress has to be laid.

As far as the Judeo-Western monotheists are concerned the apparent absurdity of their eschatology ('eternal' heavens and hells; creatures and states having a beginning but no end; relative acts bringing absolute consequences etc.) can precisely be explained by a wish to concentrate all the energy at man's disposal on his immediately apparent last ends (therefore without seeming to come out of the human sphere). These doctrines wish at all costs to avoid cramping or dispersing man's efforts by raising considerations that are inopportune in practice given the prevalent psychological conditions of the section of humanity in question: there is always to be found, both in the stressings and the reticencies of the traditional teachings, an initial aim of edging man in the direction that best suits his nature, calling into play the means which that nature also comprises, even if strictly speaking the professed aim only applies to the earlier stages of his spiritual way.

Human logic derives from the Divine Wisdom and not inversely; the 'divine logic' may therefore follow patterns which totally elude the ordinary understanding of man and of which the differences between religions – irreconcilable outwardly – provide examples which are even more disconcerting than any of those apparent inconsistencies within a selfsame sacred text such as constitute a common stumbling-block for the religious doubter. The 'mythological wording' of any traditional perspective is essentially determined by a spiritual and social interest which in an ultimate sense coincides with the truth; this it does by definition. The sacred wording contains in its own way the infinite Truth, failing which it could not serve an interest that is concerned with that Truth and indeed with nothing else.

CHAPTER VII

MORE ABOUT HUMAN DESTINIES
THE FUNCTION OF MERCY

FROM the preceding discussion of the various eschatologies, whether Buddhist or Judeo-Christian or otherwise, it should have become plain that such doctrines can never entirely accommodate their contents to human understanding. Take for example the associated Gospel statements that 'scandal must come' but that 'woe unto him by whom scandal cometh': read together, these two statements place an impossible strain on ordinary logic which, by definition, is incapable of reconciling realities that contradict one another, for much the same reason as the eye is incapable of fixing its gaze on two different planes at once; but this fact does not warrant our denying that our own limitations exist or claiming that Revelation has been wrong in expressing itself thus; even the physical realm shows us examples of antinomies that are rationally irreducible. We are forced to believe that space and time are limitless – the hypothesis of a spacial limit to extension or of a temporal limit to duration being *per se* contradictory – but we are not able to imagine it; that we should be able to represent to ourselves a situation where, after traversing all space, we would find ourselves back at our point of departure solves nothing from the point of view of concrete imagination. Space is 'round', therefore it is limited, but not spacially limited; it would be impossible to arrive at its confines otherwise than in an indirect way, given the fact that our faculties of sensation cannot under any circumstances come outside the spacial condition. As for time, it is 'spiroidal' and irreversible, hence its cyclic rhythm.

The upshot of all this is that on the physical plane we needs must 'believe' something apparently absurd and this, despite our own incapacity to grasp it in an immediate manner; for the absence of a limit in the case of a dimension that is measurable in itself is an absurdity, but the fact is that the very data of the problem impose this conclusion upon us. But if this is true of the physical realm, then by what right will we summarily deny the apparent contradictions in the metaphysical realm as propounded by Revelation? We simply have to resign ourselves to the fact that human reason has its limits, just like our faculties of sensation which are the first to commit illogicalities: they commit them in function of the existential prejudice represented by the *ego*, the subject. As for pure Intellect, it escapes these limits 'from within' even while being compelled, externally and on the plane of formulations, to espouse the contours of reasoning and language – the Buddha when communicating the liberating truths to men could not help using the language associated with human thought, failing which he would have had to remain silent; it is however a radically false opinion to take this fact as a means of demonstrating that intellection as such belongs to the same order of reality as profane thinking. What the Intellect really allows us to grasp is the 'limited illimitation' of space and time and the internal homogeneity of the universal antinomies, but it does not allow us to 'see' these things or to assimilate them in human fashion, so to speak; Existence will always comprise, for man as such, an element of 'scandal' or mystery.

Once again let it be said, the enigmas offered by the Holy Scriptures are neither less understandable nor more absurd for the rational mind than the absence of limitation characterizing the existential conditions in which we live; one meets the antinomy between necessity and liberty, or between ontological 'good' and the 'evil' which incidentally results from it, in all the traditional doctrines though expressed in differing terms.

Now, if we start out from the idea that, metaphysically speaking, there is no evil properly so called and that all is simply a question of function or aspect we shall then have to specify on the following lines: an evil being is a necessary fragment of a larger good or an element of an equilibrium which exceeds that being incommensurably whereas a good being is a good in itself, so that any evil in the latter is but fragmentary. Evil, then, is the fragment of a good and the good is a totality that includes evil and neutralizes it by its very quality of totality.

One question which gives rise to many difficulties in the consciousness of present-day man is that of damnation, even when this idea is rendered less absolute by the metaphysical reservations that impose themselves: how can a human being merit such a penalty and what interest can Heaven have in his chastisement? The answer is that immortality, whatever may be its contents (or its risks) is the measure of the quasi-divine majesty of man: *noblesse oblige*. It is, to say the least, strange that men who are most jealous about their own autonomy, whether real or illusory, ask to be treated like irresponsibles as soon as there is any question of paying the debts incurred in the exercise of the liberty they are so proud of. Before Heaven that reveals norms and utters commandments, man makes a great point of his own freedom and independence, logically therefore he admits his own responsibility; but he declares himself to be irresponsible and throws back the blame on nature and destiny, in other words on God ('it is not I that created the world') the minute Heaven begins to speak of judgment or whenever there is the least question of 'concordant reactions', of immanent justice, of *karma*. One thing that should at least cause one to think but which pride, simulating intelligence, prevents people from taking into consideration, is the fact that men for thousands of years and without undue difficulty have accepted the idea of posthumous punishments, a fact that can be explained by their still having kept a sufficient sense of the godlike majesty of the human species. They felt that there is something absolute about the state of man and that heavenly Justice knows us better than we know ourselves and also that it cannot fail to make due allowance for any genuine irresponsibility comprised in our nature.

Modern man, on the other hand, lives below himself and would fain impose on Heaven his own evaluation of the human condition, arbitrary and convenient as this is; he would like, as Voltaire put it, 'to sit under his own fig-tree and eat his own bread without asking himself what there is inside it.' Now, in order to do this, there is no need to be a man; the least of animals accomplishes this much without difficulty. It is our theomorphic nature that dictates for us our behaviour; our real nature is that which God asks of us, or that which, in the sight of the Absolute, is our true destiny. The fact that the best of mankind (to put it mildly) have never stopped short at eating their bread under a fig-tree while asking themselves no questions proves that the Voltairian man is mistaken, that his dream is unrealizable and engages no one else but himself; since Plato, Virgil and St Augustine have existed (not to mention the Sages of Asia) it can no longer be said, of man, that he is a goat or an ant.

It is undeniable that modern man has lost the sense of sin; where, in former times, people would have said 'we are sinners, incapable, insufficient', today they blithely declare that 'religion is bankrupt'. Where previously a man would say 'I am not intelligent enough to understand Thomism' (one is now thinking of the Christian world) today he will say that 'Thomism is out of date' and so forth indefinitely. The kind of attitude in question can best be described by saying that man no longer has a feeling of his own smallness and that consequently he has become insensitive to all the manifold violations brought about through the debasing of his nature, in short that he has become too pleased with himself to have any longer a clear consciousness of the ambiguity attaching to his own condition. Moreover the above remark does not run counter to what was said above about man's intrinsic majesty, for the actual smallness of man is one thing, a smallness not of right but of fact though become relatively 'real' because of a global fall from Grace, and another thing is the smallness that man attributes artificially to himself and in which he wallows in order to escape the terrors of his own divinity: this whole attitude might well be called man's illusion of a 'spiritual extraterritoriality' whereby he feels dispensed from heeding the warning voice of *karma* or, in Christian terms, the Will of God. To the empty shadow of his neglected human consciousness man then gives the name of 'anguish' and this fills him with hatred for all those who, still possessing this consciousness and accepting the positive responsibilities implied therein, escape this anguish and for this very reason feel no impulse to revolt against the dictates of religion; these two complexes, anguish and revolt, the so-called humanist would fain make universal, for it is in the very nature of man not to wish to go to perdition all alone.

Human responsibility can be total, but not absolute; it is this that explains the intervention of the divine Mercy; the latter is amply sufficient to satisfy the argument of our fragility. There is a point where man is always entirely responsible: this is when he refuses Mercy; this refusal, which echoes the pride and fall of Lucifer, is that which most surely brings about a lapse into the infernal states. That which really judges us is our own norm that we carry within ourselves and which is at once an image of the whole Cosmos and of the divine Spirit shining at its centre; whether that judgment be personified as Yama, as in the traditional representation of the Round of Existence according to the Buddhist iconography or else in some other manner, as on the portal of Chartres for instance, it amounts to the same thing doctrinally: our own *karma* rewards or condemns us. The impious man thinks all he has to do in order to escape that norm is to shut his eyes and pretend not to be human, in a word, to live below his own real level; in his wish not to know that to be a man means to pass through the narrow gate, he refuses the very Mercy that is trying to open a passage for him.

The metaphysical importance of Mercy is all the more apparent from the fact that Buddhism, while being non-theistic and thus seeming to abandon man to his own initiative and to the logic of an ineluctable *karma*, nevertheless has developed a whole mythology of Compassion, if one may so say: nowhere is this particular feature more strongly accentuated or expressed under more varied forms than in the Buddhist tradition; a whole method of prayer and confidence exists to give effect to the same idea, culminating in the Pure Land doctrine associated with the Name of Amitābha Buddha in which Mercy even takes on, in conformity with its own nature, the aspect of a personal and redemptive Divinity; if at first sight this seems a paradoxical result where Buddhism is concerned, it really involves no contradiction of principle, as anyone who examines the way in which this particular spiritual method is presented can see for himself.

In a certain sense, the divine Mercy is the normal measure of human relativity. To accept that mercy is like the peak of our own ability to choose well or ill, and it is the complement of intelligence in the work of our liberation.

CHAPTER VIII

WHAT IS MATTER
AND WHO IS MĀRA?

MATTER, as was pointed out before, is nothing else but the extreme limit or precipitation-point in the process of manifestation, at least for our world; consequently, it is the 'lowest' thing to be found within that reality that concerns us. It might nevertheless be asked whether this lowest thing is not on the contrary a 'consciousness' of sorts, namely the principle of evil, that Māra who tempted the Buddha or Satan who tempted Christ? This difficulty is resolved however, if one distinguishes in the Cosmos two poles, the one existential, blind and passive and the other intellectual, therefore conscious and active: matter is the point of precipitation in relation to the existential pole only, while the intellectual pole gives rise, at the extreme limit of the process of flight from God, to that 'personifiable force', or that perverted consciousness, who is Satan or Māra. In other words, Matter is the existence most remote from pure Being, and the Devil is the consciousness most remote from pure Intelligence, the divine Intellect; and since on the intellectual plane this remoteness can only spell subversion or opposition, that intelligence which is most remote from the Absolute will be the one that denies the Absolute as 'intelligibly', or rather as consciously, as possible. Existence – the *materia secunda* or *natura naturata* of the medieval Schoolmen, opposed by them to *Natura naturans* or divine Prototype – in course of drawing away from pure Being becomes 'hardened' and at the same time segmented: Matter is the most 'weighted' and the most 'broken' existence of all – regarded from the human point of view, be it understood, since assuredly there can be worlds other than ours, implying other limits of manifestation; while Māra is the most subversive possible intelligence, the most perverse; as compared with Māra, however, matter though hardened and corrupted remains innocent.

Howbeit, we must not make the mistake of confusing stupidity with satanism or vulgarity with mere materiality. There is a consciousness that is diminished through contact with the pole of matter and this is unintelligence, human or other; and there is an existence enhanced through contact with the pole of intelligence (if indirectly) and this is the nobility of material substances, whether of noble metals and precious stones or, passing through the vegetable order, the bodily beauty of living things. Intelligence, in the process of drawing away from the Self, is not necessarily diabolical, it can sink passively, becoming diminished without subversion. Likewise existence, in drawing away from Being, is not exclusively hardness and undifferentiated inertia; it can be accompanied by qualities that bring it near to the pole of 'Spirit' and in this sense it is not far-fetched to say of the diamond or of a flower that it displays more intelligence than such and such a stupid man. The power to teach inherent in the things of Nature, especially when in her virgin state, is bound up with this qualitative possibility attaching to natural things: for the North American Indians wild Nature is their Book of the Scriptures rendering all written texts needless in their tradition and even writing as such; all that is wanted is the science enabling them to read the signs;[1] by comparison, urbanized and sophisticated man has become largely blind and his opportunities to learn from his surroundings have been catastrophically reduced in practice.

Before proceeding further and even at some risk of repetition, let us once again go into the question of the limitation of matter and of such science as would confine itself to matter; or (what comes to the same) the question of the reality that lies 'behind' the material plane. Modern science, by its own showing, remains strictly horizontal and linear; at no point does it reach above and beyond the plane of sensible manifestation. When speaking of 'science', the author has in mind the general scientific outlook,

---

[1] Islam attributes a similar illuminative function to the various signs (*ayat*) of Nature: the nomad of the Arabian desert and his fellow of the North American prairie have shared this truth, each in his own way.

which is based principally on the physical sciences; psychology belongs on this same level, moreover, inasmuch as it does not include the recognition of one or more supra-sensorial dimensions, in the sense of concrete and objective realities and not merely in the sense of psychological dreams. It must be added that for those who do accept these dimensions – some anthropologists or ethnologists for instance – an unequivocal rejection of psycho-analytical speculations is of the utmost importance.

Magic for example, be it 'white' or 'black', enters into a supra-sensorial (but in no case transcendent) dimension, a dimension of 'depth' as one might say: the point about magic is that it does not, like official science, confine itself to reducing material phenomena to 'energies' or 'movements' of a more or less physical character includable, that is to say, in the post-paradisial solidification of the terrestrial or spacial substance;[1] but it bypasses the material shell 'in the direction of the interior' by entering into the underlying subtle or *animic* substance: hence the power to 'dematerialize' and transform displayed by *Shamans* and other practitioners of magic, be it of a benign or of an evil kind. This power, despite the much evidence, is denied by official science, which fails to perceive the subtle intermediary linking the seemingly contradictory phenomena of magical trans-locations and metamorphoses. This same science fails to perceive, *a fortiori*, the dimension of 'height' any more than that of 'depth', that is to say the Spiritual World, concerning which magic can also remain in ignorance; now it is this spiritual dimension that explains theurgic action and miracles. From the standpoint of this latter dimension, the subtle or animic order, that which both magical science and spiritualistic empiricism[2]

[1] In *The Reign of Quantity and the signs of the times* by René Guénon (Luzac, 1953) is to be found a clear explanation of the *qualitative* inequality of temporal phases or periods of history. This doctrine is of the highest importance and this is doubtless why it is side-tracked, with a sort of infallible instinct, by all the modernistically minded representatives of religion of both West and East, who evidently have a strong motive for prefering equivocal explanations concerning the possibilities of the age they live in, given the fact that they already believe dogmatically in an integral and indefinite progress.

[2] This latter empiricism is one that operates blindly, being linked with a false doctrine into the bargain; but this fact does not in itself prevent this type of phenomenon from being real at its own level. Here one has to distinguish between certain given phenomena and the quite false explanations wished onto them.

deal with, is 'a shell' in its turn, just as matter is a shell from the standpoint of the subtle world. By way of illustration the subtle substance might perhaps best be compared to a heavy liquid like blood, and the spiritual or supra-formal substance to air or a gas.

Metaphysically, it is necessary to add yet another dimension: the divine or nirvānic dimension whereof the spiritual dimension is but the cosmic reflexion or 'angelic' emanation. In the most diverse traditional symbolisms the three dimensions described above are respectively represented by 'earth', 'fire' and 'light'.

When speaking of Matter, one is not oblivious of the fact that from the Buddhist point of view it tends to be regarded in a subjective and empirical sense chiefly: but this fact does not essentially affect the question we have been discussing; the fact that Matter may only interest some people in its capacity of a phenomenon of consciousness is itself independent of the relatively objective content of that phenomenon as such.

*

There is much to be said about the close and almost complementary relationship between matter and the *ego*. The one factor evokes the other: matter, in all its weightiness, opacity and separativity is that which, in a final analysis, has been decreed by individuation: to a pseudo-Self there corresponds a pseudo-Being, which in its turn determines the soul, attracting, hardening and dissipating it at the same time. Pure intelligence transcends both matter and the *ego*; to postulate a relationship between intelligence as such and the sin of pride, as has so often happened in Christian circles, is to lay down a contradiction in terms, the intellectual element being really at the antipodes of that lived illogicality that is called 'me', as also of that blind and deadly coagulation we call 'matter'; it is in the very nature of the intellect to correct the optical illusion of the individuality and to break free from the deceptiveness of earthly things. Intelligence leads us away from matter because it perceives its painful limitations – the Buddha's First Truth expresses this in principle – and this presupposes that the intelligence is not *per se* impregnated with those limitations and is therefore entirely its own self. Likewise, intelligence leads us away from the agent of illusion, the *ego*, both in virtue of its own universality and also because its own nature, for that same reason, does not admit of any possible partisan attitude towards beings or things: 'non-duality' belongs to its very substance.

As for Reason, this is intelligence intrinsically individualized while passion, for its part, is intelligence intrinsically materialized or sensualized: one has to add the word 'intrinsically' because every mental formulation, even when its contents belong to a supra-rational order, amounts to a kind of individualization, just as every pleasure of the senses, even when this is in no wise passionate but merely experienced, is in some degree a materialization of the soul, a projection into the sensible order. It is true that both reason and passion can be turned in the direction of God; nevertheless it is not reason that is going to comprehend God nor passion that is going to reach Him: reason must first allow itself to be enlightened by the divine Intellect to the point of perceiving its own limits through a direct act of knowledge, while passion, for its part, needs to be transmuted, by Mercy, into a supernatural love.

If metaphysically all is 'empty', this means cosmologically and by way of consequence that all must needs return to the Void; the whole Buddhist method derives from this truth. After all, is there anything more self-contradictory than this blending of life and death that makes our world? Living death and dying life: here is the whole terrestrial condition and, like all contradictions moreover, this dilemma cries out for a solution on a superior plane and in fact on the same plane out of which it proceeded during the process of crystallization from below. This means, in effect, that matter will have to be reabsorbed into its celestial source like a wave which, having reached the limit of its expansion, falls back from the shore; matter must return to pure Life. This simile allows one to sense what is meant by the 'naturally miraculous' transmutation known in theology as the 'resurrection of the body' where 'death is swallowed up in victory (or in life)', as St Paul put it.[1]

[1] The unusual expression 'naturally miraculous' calls for explanation: the 'miraculous' is that which is due to a direct or 'vertical' intervention of a heavenly Power, and not to a 'horizontal' progression of causality. If one extends the notion of 'nature' to all that exists, miracles are natural like everything else, but in that case words would become meaningless, as it would then

The grand reabsorption of the sensible world – not implying the least fusion – will be heralded by cataclysms on a cosmic scale which will be like the cracking of the shell of our existence; matter, by passing through the fire, will be vapourized, not in the physical sense of the word (which would in no wise take us out of the material world), but in the sense that it will be 'discomposed towards the interior', as it were, that is to say in the direction of the subtle and principial order and will rejoin, in due course, the protomatter of the terrestrial Paradise, that of the non-evolutive creation of species. Moreover death, for the human microcosm, is none other than this same regression, for the macrocosm; herein is to be seen the distinction between a 'particular judgment' and the 'general judgment'. In both cases, man has every interest in keeping himself watchful and ready; as an old German proverb has it 'he who dies before dying, dies not when he dies'. Man in dying needs to be at the level of his new condition, failing which he will be clothed in the very form of his own insufficiency or of his own internal contradiction or, shall we say, of his 'sin': his separation from his own norm or prototype will then make itself felt as an inextinguishable fire.

The following quotation from the *Bhagavadgita* (XVI. 4) puts the position with particular clearness: 'hypocrisy, arrogance, vanity, fury, insolence and ignorance belong to him who is born, oh Partha, for a demoniac destiny'. According to Shankara's commentary we are to understand by 'hypocrisy' (or ostentation) the claim to be just and without defects; by 'arrogance' is meant pride in erudition, wealth or social status; by 'insolence' is meant any statement implying that the blind see clearly or that the ugly is beautiful or, in other words, a contempt for truth, falsification of facts, inversion of normal relationships; lastly 'ignorance' means a false conception of our own duties.

In Judeo-Christian parlance, it is because Adam after the fall was no longer at the level of the paradisial ambiency that

---

be impossible to make the essential distinction between blind or unconscious causes and the supra-conscious Cause which is the source of all consciousness and of all power. People of scientific bent too readily confuse the miraculous with the irrational and the arbitrary.

the state of semi-death that is post-edenic matter came to be produced: we die because this matter is itself a substance of death, an accursed substance; our state is something like that of fishes unknowingly enclosed in a block of ice. According to one text of the Pāli Canon, the *Aggañña-sutta*, the progressive materialization of man and his surroundings is due to the fact that the primordial and 'prematerial' men, who formerly had shone like stars and had glided through the air and fed on Beatitude, began to eat soil at the time when the terrestrial surface emerged from the waters. This earliest earth was colourful, scented and sweet, but men, through feeding on it, lost their own radiance; then it was that the sun and moon appeared, days and nights, therefore also the external light with its alternations and its measurable duration. Later the soil itself ceased to be edible and became limited to producing edible plants; later again, only a small number of plants could be eaten and man had to nourish himself at the price of hard labouring. Passions and vices, and with them adversities, increasingly found a place in the world. Myths like this one, describing the hardening of the primordial substance, are to be found almost everywhere and constitute, like all the most basic traditional data, a testimony whereof the traces are lost in the night of centuries; this is tantamount to saying that they form part of man himself.

As for Revelation, this is a ray from the sun of Omniscience whereby we are taught that the ice in which the human fishes are now encased is not everything and that something else both surrounds and permeates the ice and that the ice in any case is not our own selfhood; Omniscience teaches us all this because it is in our nature to learn it, even as the swallows are taught to fly southwards and the plants to turn towards the light.

The religions of mankind present essential truths in the form of symbols and they have good reason, corroborated by thousands of years' experience, to present them thus. We cannot exist in opposition to Being nor can we think in opposition to Intelligence; we needs have to match our own rhythms to those of the Infinite. When we breathe, one part of the air is assimilated, another part is rejected. The same is true of the reabsorption of universal manifestation, whether regarded as a whole or in its constituent parts: only that remains close to God that conforms to His nature. Finally everything is 'breathed in' by the source of all good – a source flashing forth in power, but ever merciful.

The manifested Universe comprises two rhythms, the one horizontal and the other vertical: the cosmic cycles follow each other in an incommensurable coming and going, but all this manifestation will disappear in its turn; it will ultimately be breathed in by its immutable Cause.

CHAPTER IX

SOME FALLACIES AND FACTS CONCERNING BUDDHISM

BUDDHISM has sometimes been described as a 'philosophy' or again as a 'natural religion'. To say that Buddhism is 'natural' makes sense only if this is intended to mean that, unlike the Semitic religions, it is anchored in the existential mystery of things or is so at least under some of its aspects: the latter reservation is necessary because it would also be possible to speak of the 'intellectual mystery' of existence, to which Buddhism essentially refers, given that 'Extinction' or 'Voidness' is none other than Selfhood, a word which Buddhism, however, refrains from defining or even naming; the whole doctrine of *anātmā* is calculated to prevent any conceptual and therefore restrictive attribution from being applied to the Divine Suchness which, being free from all otherness, alone is wholly Itself.

Likewise it can be said of Buddhism that in a sense it 'extracts' the Divine from our nature even as flint produces fire: which means, precisely, that what we call 'nature' is not exclusively nature and that it does not come outside the divine mystery inasmuch as, in an ultimate analysis, 'all is *Ātmā*', as the Vedantists say. The same truth is also being expressed when certain schools of Buddhism teach that a Buddha resides at the heart of every grain of dust; other schools again render this idea by saying that 'every stone can become Buddha (enlightened)'. This same factor of 'nature' also explains not only a certain apparently 'rational' (not rationalist) character attaching to Buddhism but also the human side of the youthful Gotama's experience; this experience proves, not that Buddhism is not supernatural and supra-rational nor that Sākyamuni was not an Avatāra, but only that the Buddhist perspective possesses a certain 'naturist' (not naturalistic) character inasmuch as the way to Nirvāna starts out from the empirical nature of things.

According to the Buddha's own teaching, his doctrine, far from being a philosophical ratiocination, is on the contrary 'profound, difficult to realize, difficult to understand, ungraspable by reason'. Highly significant also is this gesture: the Buddha picks up a handful of leaves and explains to his disciples that just as these leaves are but a small thing compared to the forest, so also the doctrines he preaches are but a minute portion of what he knows; of this knowledge he will only reveal that which is useful for Deliverance; for speculation apart from this one purpose he has no use. The Buddha in fact had to demonstrate, by the unfolding of his own experience leading finally to Bodhi, Awakening, the way out of this world of suffering; to see in this a proof of imperfection, as some have done, is as illogical as to apply a similar reasoning to Jesus, who let himself be baptized and who fasted in the wilderness even while 'being God'.

The rationalizing aspect of the Buddhist dialectic here calls for two observations, though some might regard this as a digression from our main subject: firstly, the Eastern wisdom does not only reside in its doctrinal formulations, whereof the apparent simplicity easily calls forth the contempt of the philosophical mind, but it resides also, and essentially, in the way these formulations are envisaged and their whole contents assimilated; in order to understand the value of any form of wisdom it is evidently necessary to know how to place oneself at the viewpoint of those to whom its message is addressed and to possess the intelligence – or the kind of intelligence – it presupposes. The second observation is as follows: there exists no proof, not indeed of the supernatural as such, but of a particular supernatural treated as unique and exclusive; if it be objected, by persons hostile to Buddhism, that the Buddhist claim to the supernatural, or in other words to the divine origin of the Buddha's message and to its efficacy for salvation, may itself be only an illusion, intelligence being only a 'human thing' and the miraculous not amounting in itself to proof, the answer is that this is a two-edged argument, since it is always possible to make a logical case – materialists do not fail to do so – for treating the alleged proofs of divinity simply as a vast objectivation of purely human wishfulness; one can always argue that the keys to the evidence are illusory, that even the eye can be deceived and that nothing ever amounts to certainty. There then remains only the certitude of Grace; but if this argument is irrefutable in one case (the Christian case, for instance) it is equally so in the case of those foreign perspectives that this kind of argument is used to discredit.

But there is yet another side to this question: out of a wish to cash in, from apologetic motives this time, on the 'purely natural' and 'non-obscurantist' character of Buddhism, modernistic champions (Eastern as well as Western) of the Buddhist tradition itself like to point out that the reality of Buddhahood resides only 'in our mind': here again is to be seen an evolutionist distortion of an esoteric datum, for these people carefully avoid saying that here the interior transcendence of the human mind is in question or, in a final analysis, the nature of selfhood and not just some mental fiction or other. If to be Buddha is identical with Selfhood, it is doubly evident that the Buddha is our mind, in the sense that there can be no Intellect apart from him. At the same time (this is another aspect of the same question) the Buddha appears in our intelligence as a concept, but for which he would be ungraspable so that we would not be able to think or speak of him in any way. Obviously one can say that this Buddha, not being Buddhahood as such but only a provisional and inevitable inkling thereof, dwells in our mind like any other concept: this means, not that the Buddha does not possess a relatively objective, or shall we say 'supra-subjective' reality outside us, but simply that we ourselves are incapable, with our false feeling of plenitude that we take for self, to grasp in a direct way the 'self-nature' of Buddhahood.

*

Seeing that there is an allusion, in the preceding paragraph, to the evolutionist prejudice, it is surely permissible to say a few more words on the subject: evolutionism would be justified if a tree could produce something other and better than what is contained in its seed; it would be justified if the fruits of the tree were, not the manifestation of that which the seed already contains, but the result of an unpredictable development, variable according to circumstances, or if it were a matter of chance whether an apple tree shall give apples and not figs. The phenomena of evolution and transmutation assuredly exist within the limits of certain contingencies, otherwise the seed would never become a tree and a plant would never modify its shape under given conditions, such as a change of soil or climate; nevertheless these two factors, evolution and trans-mutation, remain quite secondary in relation to the principle of qualitative anticipation of effects within their own cause. These truths assume a particular importance when there is question of Revelations and traditions, for the slightest error on this plane is devastating to the soul and to the intelligence.

This provides an opportunity to point out another prejudice common to the modernist and evolutionist mind and hence totally contrary to authentic Buddhism, namely the claim to a maximum of 'freedom' for the human animal or, in other words, the ideal of a quasi-total absence of constraints in respect of man when considered apart from his content or quality and also apart from his metaphysical finality; now the only freedom proportioned to our nature is that which opens the gates towards the eternal Freedom we all carry in the depths of our being, the possibility which objectively may be known as Enlightenment and subjectively as Buddhahood; it is senseless to give the name of freedom, as is persistently done by our so-called 'thinkers', to that which hands over man's weakness – especially collective man's – to the powers of dissolution and spiritual suicide. To give an instance from the Hindu tradition, the Brahmin, when remaining true to his vocation, is at once the most independent and the most obedient of men; which means that he who is socially the freest must be inwardly the most bound – liberation through Knowledge excepted. Two things are certain: firstly, that in an integral society everyone cannot be free, or rather everyone cannot be free in the same way; and secondly, that a society, like a cosmos, cannot avoid the approximations and errors that spring from its condition: that is to say, there will always be exceptions positive or negative, miracles or abuses. It is only on the spiritual plane that the pure norms, and with them perfect justice, are to be found. When spirituality has become darkened it is vain to wish to establish an ideal justice, this being impossible to implant among men who are themselves devoid of justice; and it is still more vain to seek to establish justice at the expense of principles which, though badly applied in fact, are nevertheless the only application of justice that is concretely possible in a given human ambience.[1]

On any legitimate showing, one can adapt a traditional principle to meet new circumstances in such measure as these are unavoidable, but one cannot reject that principle in its very substance.

[1] The abuses of the French Revolution – to cite but one instance – were certainly not less than those of the monarchy in its decadence, indeed quite the contrary; instead of throwing overboard the monarchical and theocratic principles, these should have been given back their full sense, which was a religious one; this is just what the nobility neglected to do since the Renaissance. If one wishes to maintain people in the faith, or to maintain a popular balance founded on faith, one has to prove that one is in possession of faith oneself; injustice towards the people, and the consequent injustice of the people in regard to those who represent higher principles if imperfectly, always springs from a previous injustice in respect of God.

CHAPTER X

GLIMPSES INTO ZEN

THE interest in Zen manifested of late years in the Western countries has resulted from an understandable reaction against the coarseness and ugliness prevalent in the world today, and also from a certain weariness in regard to concepts rightly or wrongly judged to be inoperative; while on the other hand people have tended to feel increasingly bored by the habitual philosophical battles of words. Unfortunately, these justifiable motives get only too easily mingled with anti-intellectual and falsely 'concretist' tendencies – this was only to be expected – in which case the reaction becomes deprived of all effective value. For it is one thing to take up a stand beyond the scope of the thinking faculty and another to remain far short of that faculty's highest possibilities even while imagining one has transcended things of which one does not comprehend the first word. He who truly rises above verbal formulations will ever be ready to respect those which have given direction to his thinking in the first place; he will not fail to venerate 'every word that proceedeth out of the mouth of God'. There is a rustic proverb which says that only the pig overturns its trough after emptying it and the same moral is to be found in the well-known fable of the fox and the grapes. If Zen is less given to doctrinal formulation than other schools, this is because its own structure allows it to be so; it owes its consistency to factors that are perfectly rigorous, but not easily grasped from the outside; its silence, charged with mystery, is quite other than a vague and facile mutism. Zen, precisely by reason of its direct and implicit character, which is admirably suited to certain possibilities of the Far Eastern mind, presupposes so many conditions of mentality and environment that the slightest lack in this respect jeopardizes the result of any effort however sincere; at the same time we must not forget that a typical man of the Japanese *élite* is in many respects a product of Zen.

But there is also an inverse danger, this time affecting Far Eastern people themselves: followers of Zen (as also Theravādins in a different way) in the course of their scholastic and academic contacts with the West find it hard to resist making capital of what is, in a sense, the adogmatic character of their own tradition, as if the absence of dogmas bore the same meaning and colour for a contemplative Asiatic as for a Western agnostic. Similar misunderstandings have also been apparent in the realm of art, where contemporary 'abstract' productions have been confused, in Japan, with works inspired by Tao-Zen, at least as regards their intention. With this can be compared the confusion persistently fostered by European psychologists as between drawings by insane patients and Tantrik Buddhist *māndalas;* in the latter case, just as in the case of the Zen 'adogmatism', appearances are equated which in reality are at the antipodes of one another and this, moreover, is precisely the reason why they are thus confused.[1]

In a quite general way, that which calls for suspicion and for an implacable vigilance is the reducing of the spiritual to the psychic, a practice which by now has become a commonplace to the point of characterizing Western interpretations of the traditional doctrines. This so-called 'psychology of spirituality' or this 'psychoanalysis of the sacred' is the breach through which the mortal poison of modern relativism infiltrates into the still living Oriental traditions. According to Jung the figurative emergence of certain contents of the 'collective unconscious' is accompanied empirically, as its psychic complement, by a noumenal sensation of eternity and infinitude. This is the way to ruin insidiously all transcendence and all intellection for, according to this theory, it is the collective unconscious, or subconscious, which is at the origin of 'individuated' consciousness, human intelligence having two

[1] In one encyclopaedia dealing with Japan (*Le Japon illustré* Paris, 1915) is to be found the following sentence intended to comfort Western readers: '. . . this neo-Buddhism has ceased to be an ultra-metaphysical, ascetic, anti-natural religion; it is a kind of lay religion, purely moral and justified by its national and social advantages.' All is there, nothing is missing! And thanks for the commendation.

components, namely the reflexions of the subconscious on the one hand and the experience of the external world on the other; but since experience is not in itself intelligence, on this showing intelligence will have the sub-conscious for its substance, so that one has to try and define the sub-conscious on the basis of its own ramification. This is the classical contradiction of all subjectivist and relativist philosophy.

Assuredly, there is no question here of denying that whatever is truly spiritual, though essentially determined by supra-individual factors, will also include secondary modalities of a psychic, and even of a corporeal order from the very fact that it necessarily sets in motion 'all that we are'. Granted that this is so, a 'psychology of the spiritual' nevertheless is a contradictory notion that can only end up in falsifying and negating the spirit; one might just as well speak of 'a biology of truth' and indeed one can be pretty sure that someone has already done so. In an analogous way, many people are apt to confuse what is supra-logical with the illogical and vice versa: as soon as a, to them, uncomfortable demonstration is found to be logically faultless, these people hasten to write it off as 'aristotelian' or 'cartesian' in order to stress the artificial and outmoded character they fain would attribute to it.

When referring to the much canvassed 'non-dogmatism' of the Buddhist teachings one has to be extremely cautious how one expresses this thought, since it is useless to lay down, out of contempt for dogmatic forms, conditions that could never in fact be fulfilled or to let oneself be involved in conclusions which may be quite logical in form perhaps, but which are erected on false bases, contrary to reality. One can never cease wondering at the levity with which some people, in their scorn of all dogmas for reasons allegedly spiritual, forget to consult tradition concerning such and such an order of possibilities while blithely claiming that their little personal *recipe* is at long last going to inaugurate a new world where all will be happy even if they be plunged in illusion – when the Buddha himself did not succeed in accomplishing this, even supposing he had wished to do so. Apart from the sheer inanity of such a pretension, one finds here a fundamental ignorance regarding the qualitative differences of historical phases; these people wish to lay down the law about things situated in the Universe without having the least notion of the laws whereby it is governed and with a complete contempt of the traditions that reveal those laws. The non-dogmatism of Zen and kindred spiritualities in reality is chiefly aimed at the mental crystallizations of partial truths; it in no wise confers a general mandate against Truth as such; if it closes the door, as it does, against any fixation in a half-truth, this does not mean that it leaves the door open for every error. For the modernistically minded neo-Zen exponent, on the other hand, this same non-dogmatism becomes a licence to do anything one pleases and this, in the name of a tradition to which, if he be a Japanese, he himself remains attached atavistically and sentimentally; the sheer want of imagination sometimes displayed by persons who seem in other respects intelligent is one of the more baffling and all too common symptoms of the semi-Europeanized East.

According to the *Lankāvatara-sūtra* the being who has entered into the state of a Buddha accomplishes mysterious actions that are 'impossible to conceive' (*achintya*) and 'carried out without purpose and outside any feeling of usefulness' (*anābhoga-charyā*); this statement is poles apart from a utilitarian, not to say materialistic and demagogic Neo-Buddhism. Like other men, a Buddhist assuredly may busy himself with such and such a useful activity in response to circumstances good or bad, but only on condition he does not forget that external activities in themselves are without relation to Buddhahood and Reality; they are neither situated outside Samsāra nor opposed to illusion. More especially should it be remembered that any useful activity a man undertakes will imply the condition that he never claims to be adding anything whatsoever to tradition or to sanctity, as if these had hitherto been lacking in some essential quality which at last has been discovered thanks to Kant or Rousseau after countless centuries of insufficiency. Relativities are not things to be grafted on the Absolute.

*

Since we have been speaking about Zen it will be appropriate to add a few words about the mysterious practice conventionally known as the 'cult of tea' which, despite its rather specialized and local character, reveals an aspect of the Buddhist spirit that is far from insignificant. Contrary to the opinion of some who profess to be specialists but whose personal bias causes them to regard the 'tea-ceremony' in Japan as nothing but a rather precious social grace, certain Japanese followers of Zen have informed the author of this book that the tea-rite on the contrary carries 'a very deep meaning' – these were their own words. Tea, as they explained, here stands for the Essence and mastery in the art of tea requires that the act be accomplished, not by the *ego*, but by the Void or the Self. To prepare tea with meticulous perfection and sobriety of gesture, or with elegance, amounts to nothing by itself, though a perfect technique in regard to the act obviously is both a condition and a result of this enacted symbolism, under different relationships: if one famous master, in answer to a disciple who claimed to know how to do a thing as simple as preparing tea, was able to say 'Then I become your disciple', this was precisely in order to convey the fact, not without irony but with a perfect logic, that this particular skill really implies a radical stripping away of the individuality, therefore something great and difficult.

Some people will not fail to object, against this esotericism of tea and others like it, that the Buddha never prepared tea, that he did not practice archery[1] or arrange flowers; the answer to this kind of objection is that, spiritually speaking, the manner of acting counts more than the material content of the act, at least in certain respects and provided the activities in question are in themselves legitimate. The Buddha, as a man, had to act, but all his actions were nevertheless instinct with the same superhuman quality, the same 'Buddha-nature'. After him, all kinds of other symbolical activities could be integrated in the tradition flowing from his Person thanks to the fact that they had been similarly practised by saints who themselves realized the nature of a Buddha totally or in a high degree and who thus

[1] Here no allusion is intended to the archery contest in which the youthful Prince Siddhartha took part, with its symbolical anticipation of the Enlightenment which he was destined, as Buddha, to realize. The above reference is to the use of Archery as a contemplative discipline, concerning which the reader will find a fine description in Eugen Herrigel's book '*Zen in the Art of Archery*' (Routledge and Kegan Paul 1953).

consecrated and 'sacralised' the activities they had respectively practised.[1]

In any case, one must not lose sight of the fact that prior to a certain time every act of life partook of the nature of a rite; it was the contrary that would have been abnormal in all the ages that one could reasonably describe as primitive. Here one must therefore envisage the case where an art already ritual in virtue of its origin has been 'reconfirmed' in a fresh light at a later date and interpreted in more explicit terms perhaps, but certainly not invented. However, since practically everything can be debased to the level of what is now called 'culture', even a spiritual art may be turned by and by into a simple aesthetic passtime, a game of virtuosity without conscious content or efficacy. Nevertheless, even such a residue of an art is better than nothing, inasmuch as it is able at least to provide a reminder of what it really is by rights and thus to suggest a whole forgotten world of the spirit to any mind that is sufficiently alert to grasp its still implicit meaning. For this reason the influence of the 'spirit of tea' in the Japanese civilization should not be underestimated even now.[2]

[1] 'The monks gathered before the image of Bodhidharma (First Patriarch of *Zen* who came to China from India in the VIth century AD) and drank tea out of a single bowl with the profound humility of a holy sacrament. It was this *Zen* ritual which finally developed into the tea-ceremony of Japan in the fifteenth century. . . . Our legends attribute the first arrangement of flowers to those early Buddhist saints who gathered flowers scattered by the storm and, in their infinite solicitude for all living things, placed them in bowls full of water . . . we see them (the master-florists) indicate the Directive Principle (Heaven) the Subordinate Principle (Earth), the Mediatory Principle (Man) and any arrangement that did not incorporate this principle in the flowers was considered sterile and dead. They also attached great importance to the art of showing a flower in its three different aspects: the formal, semi-formal and informal.' (Kakuzo Okakura: *The Book of Tea*. J. E. Tuttle, 1906). 'If then it is possible to say many things about the art of flowers, and whatever one can say about it, there always remains beyond the, to us, tangible and visible realizations, the mystery of its principle in unfathomable Being. . . . That which is at the basis of floral compositions and which must be lived in goodly fashion is in itself formless and only takes form in a visual and symbolic representation. This formless and spiritual form is precisely the "idea" of the art of flowers. There the incommensurable is merged with the visible in order to shine forth and become apparent through the modest forms of the sensible world.' (Gusty L. Herrigel: *Der Blumenweg*, Otto Wilhelm Barth-Verlag, 1957.)

[2] 'Manifold indeed have been the contributions of the tea-masters to art. They completely revolutionized the classical architecture and interior decora-

This question of the 'tea-cult' provides an occasion for observing, in quite a general way, that the now widespread contempt for 'the picturesque' is basically aimed against form as such, against the human eye in its primordial function, against images in their capacity of 'natural sacraments'; this goes hand in hand with contempt for speech and the word. In both cases it is, in short, a devaluing or profanation of a symbol that is taking place under the double relationship of container and contents.

Zen is a wisdom that readily draws inspiration from the image, the thing seen, be it only for the reason that it claims to have originated from the vision of a flower in the hand of the Buddha.

*

The above considerations on Zen may lead people to put the question whether that school, or else some other, most faithfully reflects the original teachings of Sākyamuni. On the level of intrinsic orthodoxy this is a meaningless question, however; it is as if one were to ask which of the branches of a tree best conforms to the root. Concerning the manifold forms of historical Buddhism the only question worth asking is that of their orthodoxy or heterodoxy; all that is orthodox today, whatever form may have developed around it, was contained in Buddhism from the beginning. All orthodox Buddhism is 'the real Buddhism'; the deployment of a more or less subtle aspect of the Dharma is never an 'evolution' in the progressivist sense of the word; inspiration is not an invention any more than a metaphysical perspective is a rationalist system. With many Asian authors, the Western terms they introduce into their writings are often employed carelessly though without an erroneous intention; but in that case it is the Western reader who must be forewarned, since otherwise he will infallibly be misled by the association of ideas normally implied in the terms that have thus been carelessly borrowed from his vocabulary.

tions, and established the new style . . . to whose influence even the palaces and monasteries built after the sixteenth century have all been subject . . . all the celebrated gardens of Japan were laid out by tea-masters. . . . It is impossible, indeed, to find any department of art in which the tea-masters have not left marks of their genius.' (Kakuzo Okakura, *op. cit.*)

As for the Western world itself, one may recall, for instance, the case of a Christian '*avant-garde*' theologian who, out of a wish to prove that 'tradition' is the equivalent of 'progress' and not an immobilism, went so far as to maintain that St Paul, in wishing to formulate such and such truths in his Epistles, 'was compelled to invent'. His general aim doubtless was to claim 'modern progress' as an outcome of Christianity and to align in one and the same glory the Apostles and the inventors of machines, serums and explosives. In the same line of thought, when a man is not intelligent enough to understand what St Thomas and the Scholastics were trying to say, this is called 'being in tune with one's own time'; while to deceive oneself thus regarding one's own intellectual obtuseness by making of it a norm will doubtless be described as 'humility'.[1]

To declare that the primitive Dharma was merely 'practical' and not 'speculative' – the *sūtras* are there to prove the contrary – amounts to reducing the Dharma to an individual experience devoid of any possibility of further radiation. Knowledge of a doctrine cannot be rendered fully adequate except on the basis of the notions of orthodoxy and tradition.

One has heard it said that Buddhism, just as it needed at a certain moment in its history to find a 'new form', namely the Mahāyāna, should in our day likewise 'be rejuvenated' consonantly with 'the spirit of the age', a statement – need one say it? – which is false twice over: firstly, because the Mahāyāna was not concocted by men nor did it seek to make itself acceptable to any 'age' whatsoever, and secondly because it constitutes, for that humanity to which its message was addressed, a definitive expression of Buddhism, valid therefore till the end of the world and the coming of Maitreya.

[1] A similar phenomenon is observable in the Catholic world as indeed in many other places. Without stopping to ask what is the value of this pseudo-absolute they call 'our own age', without even considering its tendencies, its structures, its situations, in short without putting the question whether a world without God or hostile to God can be accepted as a normal or even as a good world, some people decree without more ado that it is for religion to change, that religion must become social-minded, existentialist and surrealist in order to match the 'high level' of development attained by present-day humanity; they quite forget to consider this question the other way round and according to the normal order of relationships. Truly we are living in a world with no sense of measure.

If our age, not because of its hypothetical superiority, but on the contrary because of its misery, requires a certain readaptation of the Eternal message, this has been effected long since: Jōdo, Pure Land, is the last utterance, providential and infinitely merciful, of this message and as it addresses itself to those who are most miserable nothing could exceed it in timeliness. The man of our time can lay claim to no spiritual originality unless it be a superabundance of distress, to which the answer will be, by way of compensation, a secret outpouring of Graces, always provided that man does not close himself from beforehand to the celestial offer to save him. The greatest of all human miseries is a refusal to lay oneself open to Mercy.

PART II

BUDDHISM'S ALLY IN JAPAN SHINTŌ OR THE WAY OF THE GODS

CHAPTER XI

SCIENCE, MYTH AND THE MEANING OF ANCESTORS

It is recorded of the Emperor Shōmu that in the year 742 AD he sent an envoy to Ise shrine, symbolical centre for the nation of Japan, to request an oracle from the Sun Goddess concerning his projected building of the great Buddhist temple Tōdaiji at Nara; a favourable oracle was granted. Soon after that the Emperor had a dream in which the Goddess herself appeared to him saying 'This is the land of the Gods, the people should revere them. In my essence I am the (solar) Buddha Vairōchana. Let my people understand this and take refuge in the Law of the Buddhas'. By this token was affirmed the essential identity of the primitive tradition of Japan, Shintō, and what might otherwise have passed for a foreign importation from Korea and China, namely Buddhism: the Japanese civilization that evokes our wonder and love can be said to stem, both structurally and in its peculiar genius, from this traditional synthesis.

Many other stories have been handed down couched in a similar vein: for instance it is reported of Hōnen, the great saint who founded the Jōdo (Pure Land) school of Buddhism in Japan, that a man who afterwards became his disciple had been expressly directed to him by the Shintoist god Hachiman at whose shrine he had been praying to be shown a way of salvation. When Hōnen was exiled at the instance of those who opposed his new teachings it was the same god who eventually recommended the authorities to rescind the sentence. The chief point of all this is that there has been assimilation of the two traditional influences at one level and maintenance of their separate character at another and this is the position prevailing in Japan to this day. Whoever takes an interest in Japanese Buddhism for any reason should therefore know something of

Shintō and vice versa, otherwise many things will fail to explain themselves for want of the necessary keys.

Some might, however, be minded to ask what degree of reality attaches to this assimilation of two traditions of such very different origin. This question is, in fact, an important one inasmuch as it allows one to call attention to a particular trait of the Far Eastern mentality which the religious exclusiveness habitual in the West may find hard to appreciate at its just value. The passage from one Asiatic tradition to another – Hinduism, Buddhism, Taoism – is but a small thing, seeing that the metaphysical content is everywhere clearly apparent and even throws into relief the relativity of 'mythological' diversities; these traditions, precisely because of their spiritual transparence, even absorb foreign traditional elements quite readily; the Shintoist divinity becomes a Bodhisattva without altering its essence, since the (respective) names cover universal realities:[1] which remark brings us to a point where we may fittingly embark on our survey of the tradition to which, prior to the arrival of Buddhism and later in association with it, Providence entrusted the task of forging the Japanese soul.

*

The question of the spiritual sense underlying the myths is one of those which people gladly relegate to the realm of feeling and imagination and which 'exact science' refuses to treat otherwise than through the medium of psychological and historical conjectures.[2] For those of us, however, who disbelieve in the efficacy of a knowledge isolated from the truth as a whole (unless it be a mere matter of knowing physical things,

[1] This last sentence occurs in another work by the present author: *Sentiers de Gnose* (La Colombe, Paris 1957). An English translation of this book under the title *Gnosis, Divine Knowledge* has been published by John Murray, London, 1959: the opening chapter, from which the above quotation is taken, discusses the problem of assimilations and oppositions between religious forms in considerable detail. (*Translator's note*).

[2] Some honourable exceptions are to be found among the anthropologists of recent years, whose approach to the peoples and the folklore they study in various parts of the world is neither patronizing nor hampered by an ingrained rationalist or materialist prejudice: in short they take into accont the spiritual dimension of man, at least in some degree. However, the question remains open as to how far their studies are officially admitted into the category of 'exact science'.

actually palpable) a science run on these lines suffers precisely from this, namely that it is prone to substitute 'exactness' for intelligence, let this be said plainly; it is in effect this very exactness, practically confined as it is to the quantitative order, which stands in the way of the decisive operations of pure intelligence, just because a meticulous and often arbitrary cataloguing of facts, possibly of small significance or rendered such thanks to the point of view adopted, replaces the intellectual and qualitative perception of the nature of things. Science claims to be characterized by its refusal of all purely speculative premisses (the *voraussetzungsloses Denken* of the German philosophers) and at the same time by a complete liberty of investigation; but this is an illusion since modern science, like every other science before it moreover, cannot avoid starting out in its turn from an idea: this initial idea is the dogma concerning the exclusively rational nature of the intelligence and its more or less universal diffusion. In other words, it is assumed that there exists a unique and polyvalent intelligence (which in principle is true) and that this intelligence is possessed by everybody and furthermore that this is what allows investigation to be entirely 'free' (which is radically false). There are truths which intuitive intellection alone allows one to attain, but it is not a fact that such intellection lies within the capacity of every man of ordinarily sound mind. Moreover the Intellect, for its part, requires Revelation, both as its occasional cause and as vehicle of the 'Perennial Philosophy', if it is to actualize its own light in more than a fragmentary manner.

In any case, when people speak of 'objective analysis' they nearly always forget the principal interested party, namely the intelligence (or unintelligence) of the man who analyses; they forget that, in many cases, the analysis of facts intended to prove such and such a thing whereof the existence or non-existence is nevertheless evident *a priori* only serves to cover the absence, whether basic or accidental, of intellection and therefore of an intelligence proportioned to the magnitude of the problem as set.

When true myths are done away with, they inevitably come to be replaced by artificial myths. In practice, a mode of thought which is content to rely on its own logic alone while operating in a realm where ordinary logic opens up no vistas, thereby becomes defenceless against the various scientific mythologies of the time, rather in the same way as when religion is done away with, this leads in fact, not to a rational view of the Universe, but to a counter-religion, with its own 'faith', its dogmas, its taboos, in the name of which it will not be long before rationalism itself is eaten up. To treat man as absolutely free – man who plainly is not absolute – is to set free all manner of evils in him, without there remaining any principle whereby their propagation might be kept within bounds. All this goes to show that basically it is a kind of abuse of language to give the bare name of 'Science' to a knowledge that only leads to practical results while revealing nothing concerning the profound nature of phenomena; a science which by its own showing eschews transcendent principles can offer no sort of guarantee as to the ultimate results of its own investigations.

Pure and simple logic amounts only to a very indirect manner of knowing things; it is, before all else, the art of co-ordinating data (whether true or false) according to a given need of causal satisfaction and within the limits of a given imagination, so much so that an apparently faultless argument can yet be quite erroneous in function of the falseness of its premisses; the more elevated the order of the thing to be made known, the more vulnerable will be the mind in that case. What one is criticizing here is not the exactitude of science, far from that, but the exclusive level imposed on that exactitude, whereby this quality is rendered inadequate and inoperative: man can measure a distance by his strides, but this does not make him able to see with his feet, if one may so express oneself. Metaphysics and symbolism, which alone provide efficient keys to the knowledge of supra-sensible realities, are highly exact sciences – with an exactitude greatly exceeding that of physical facts – but these sciences lie beyond the scope of unaided *ratio* and of the methods it inspires in a quasi-exclusive manner.

*

Let it be said from the outset that if the author has felt impelled to treat here of Shintoism, the reason that originally occasioned this wish was the alleged 'abolition' of the divine status of the Japanese Emperor at the time of the American occupation; this blatant and gratuitous manifestation of the anti-traditional spirit and the characteristic folly it enshrined called as a matter of course for a study of the traditional context where the imperial prerogative fits in and whereby its claims are rendered intelligible.[1] In the pages that follow there is no question, needless to say, of going back to the Meijist falsification of the quasi-celestial dignity of the Tennō, the one that inaugurated the modernization of Japan after 1864. That period, if on the one hand it showed itself more or less hostile to Buddhism, proved no more profitable, on the other, to the genuine Shintō which it tried to pervert to nationalistic ends, after the Western model; many of Japan's more recent troubles, when viewed in retrospect, are ascribable to this initial cause.

From the standpoint of the present book, that which chiefly warrants one's including in it a subject as apparently remote as Shintō is the fact that – to paraphrase a famous saying of Philip Duke of Orleans – 'all that is traditional is ours';[2] that is to say, Truth is one, like the human species.

*

A few remarks first of all about the veneration of the dead: whenever people refer to Confucianism or Shintō they immediately think of 'ancestor-worship', coupled with a supposition that it is Ancestors who take the place of God in these traditions or, to be more exact, who function in lieu of the Divinity there, since one can only replace something that is already absent. In reality, however, the Divinity itself is conceived in the Far East as a kind of Ancestor whereof one's human ancestors are like a prolongation; or else they are seen as a bridge between ourselves and It. God is the Heaven or Sun from which we are indirectly descended and of which the Emperor is the incarnation or direct descendant, as the case may be; as for the

[1] The author is aware of the character, at once summary and loaded with detail, of the present analysis, for the subject is such as to compel one to say both too little and too much according to the way the theme is being envisaged; he wishes nevertheless to mention the encouraging fact that the late professor Chikao Fujisawa, a recognized authority in the sphere of Shintō, expressed the desire to translate this study into Japanese, a project which could not be carried out as the professor died soon after his meeting with the author.

[2] 'All that is national is ours', that is to say: belonged to the monarchists.

Sage, he is its incarnation by overwhelming necessity, according to a spiritual and 'vertical' lineage, and not a carnal and 'horizontal' lineage as in the other case.

An innate conviction that one's ancestors were 'nearer the gods' than oneself and that they incarnate something of an ideal is to be found, implicitly or in practice, among a great number even of those now professing a belief in evolutionism; many feel that the ancients, even if they make an impression of rather simple-minded beings, enjoyed 'wholeness' of character and had none of that mixture of weakness and complication, not to say corruption, that goes with the average of 'latter day' mankind. Such a conviction springs from an intuition that is natural to normal man, it is therefore related to the religious instinct; like it, it is infallible – 'prelogical', if one so prefers, but in a positive sense – that is to say this conviction arises from the very depth of our being; and by this is meant, not the chaos of our 'subconscious' but our ontological reality, coinciding with universal Intellect, without which 'was not any thing made that was made'.

If the old traditions contain stories that now seem morally and psychologically almost incomprehensible, one must say to oneself that, with the men of another age, the relationship of thought to action was much more direct than with us and also that the difference between the internal and external worlds was not yet as sharply marked as happens with the distant descendants of those men that we ourselves are; ancient man was 'more absolute' than we in all he did, more absolute in good but also more absolute in evil, or at least in certain forms of evil, for there are also some evils which only belong to the latter times. There is no call to believe, for instance, that our own Western Middle Ages were a 'good time' in a total sense, for it is just as easy to admit that it was a bad time, always provided one does so on the basis of spiritually valid criteria, neither biased in favour of the modern world that followed nor of the ancient paganism that came before.

All the saints have complained of their own time; the easy optimism in vogue today regarding the times we live in is only one more anomaly among many others. We can reproach the men of the Middle Ages with having made little use of a climate as full of spirit and hope as theirs was and with having been both too worldly and too quarrelsome; there is certainly no occasion to wonder at the great calamities that descended upon them, 'by very force of *karma*' as a Buddhist would say, since in fact the medieval worldliness already contained all the seeds of our present troubles.[1]

Many things, with the ancients, now seem to us rudimentary for the simple reason that we are unaware of what these things meant to them, with the result that we set out to judge from fragments or on the basis of appearances of a quite deceptive kind; nor must it be forgotten that a certain kind of naivety observable in earlier times was, after all, the expression of a still paradisial rightness surviving in the midst of the equivocations and paradoxes of man's earthly exile. For instance, one may note among the nomads described in the Old Testament a width of vision comprising at one and the same time the rude and the profound without needing to make much of a transition from one to the other, which is an attitude that 'civilized' man, given as he is to confusing a rational training with intelligence as such, finds it difficult to comprehend. A similar confusion attaches to many people's view of the Apostles, in the New Testament, whom they far too readily take for 'men of the people' in the trivial sense of the word and this, simply because they cannot imagine how men could be at once simple and noble, unlettered and contemplative. If the Apostles were able, for instance, to argue among themselves as to which of them would have the chief place in Paradise, they were but expressing spontaneously and directly a feeling which sophisticated man would try to keep hidden in his innermost thoughts.

[1] Maritain has observed (in his *Humanisme Intégral*) that in the Middle Ages men were deficient in respect of 'reflexive consciousness', that is to say they were but little preoccupied with their own psychic states and reactions and that, on the contrary, at the time when the Middle Ages were in decline (Ruysbroeck, Tauler), and still more after the Renaissance, this form of consciousness was much on the increase (Saint Teresa of Avila, St John of the Cross, Mary of the Incarnation). What, however, is not explained to us by the author of the above remarks is why this absence of reflexive consciousness constituted a 'deficiency' in the Middle Ages or why it made its appearance subsequently. Now what interests us most is to understand the precise cause of this change, namely the crystallizing out of individualism (which is necessarily reflexive) and of the empiricism that goes with it by way of consequence.

Among the peoples of the Far East the ancestor figures at once as the origin and as the spiritual or ethical norm; the ancestor is, for his descendants, the essential personality, that is to say the substance of which they are like the subsequent accidents; piety consists precisely in viewing the ancestor thus and in seeing in him nothing else but the bridge connecting them, his descendants, with the Divine. The patriarch is something like the 'Word made flesh' – let this be said without any abuse of language – and he is therefore what we ourselves ought to be, or what we ought to 'become' because we 'are' that thing already in principle and whereof it also behoves us to perpetuate the perfection and the glory. Ancestors are the human imprints of angelic substances and, for that reason, also of divine Qualities; to be true to them is to be true to God; they oblige us to remain in conformity with the eternal 'idea' whence we came forth, the idea which provides the law and goal of our earthly life.

This connection between the ancestor and his 'angelic' or 'divine' prototypes is clearly apparent in the Japanese word *kami*, which denotes the ancestor and also bears the implication of 'superior'; in the sacred language this word stands for 'divine aspect', 'cosmic principle', 'spirit'. The Shintō tradition itself is called *kami-no-michi* or 'Way of the Gods', which implies that it is also the way of the ancestors.

*

Possibly Shintō is the most intact and hence the most complete form belonging to a traditional current that might be described as 'Hyperborean Shamanism', one that extends across Siberia and the adjoining Mongolian lands as far as North America; many mythological and cultural concordances and even vestimentary similarities go to support such a supposition; such a parallelism contains no cause for surprise, since Mongols, Japanese and Red Indians all embody – or have embodied – the heroic side of the Yellow Race, in the broadest sense of the word. For these peoples it is above all Nature that is the sanctuary – a truth which in Japan finds concrete utterance in the *torii* placed in front of sacred landscapes – and this holiness of virgin nature and this 'transcendent immanence' is not without connexion, among the peoples concerned, with their thirst for freedom, their contempt for luxury, their taciturnness and other similar characteristics.

The likeness of the ancient Shintoist songs and those of the Red Indians is striking: 'Ho, now is the time! – Ho, now is the time! – Ho! Ha! Psha! Come on my children! – Come on my children!' (The most ancient Japanese *uta*, that has come down from the warriors of Jimmu Tennō) –'They shall appear! – May you see them! – They shall appear! – May you see them! – A horse-people appeareth. – A thunder-people appeareth. – They shall appear, look! – They shall appear, look!' (Sioux). – 'Now the rising sun – has sent his rays towards earth – coming from afar – coming from afar – coming from afar – a great number (of warriors) coming from afar, he yo!' (Pawnee) – 'Make us see, is it real? – Make us see, is it real, this life I am leading? – You, divine Beings, who abide everywhere – make us see, is it real – this life I am leading?' (Pawnee). It would not be altogether easy to guess from the mode of expression to which of the two traditions, so remote from one another geographically and historically, a given phrase belongs.

There is nevertheless in the Shintō civilization, apart from any thought of later Chinese or Buddhist influences, one element that partly separates it from the Northern Shamanist world and this is a certain degree of Malayan or Malayo-Polynesian admixture; additional causes of its originality are its insular situation, with all the psychological consequences that this entails, and also the extreme plasticity of the Yamato race, which has made of Japan a reservoir of the principal spiritual and artistic currents of Asia. All the above factors, and more besides, joined in the creating of that kind of bewitching polyphony that might well be called the 'Japanese miracle'.

To return to the analogies pointed out above, it can be said that Shintō, like the North American tradition, knows the cult of the grand phenomena of Nature: sun, moon, rain-bearing hurricane, wind, thunder and lightning, fire, wild animals, rocks, trees, not forgetting sky and earth that are their containers; above it all there is to be found, as 'Great Spirit', *Ame-no-Minakanushi-no-kami*, the 'Lord of the true Centre of Heaven'. Of this cosmology we shall speak again later.

CHAPTER XII

ETHICS AND MYTHOLOGY
OF SHINTŌ

It may occasion surprise to some that the eschatological element, prominent in most religions, apparently plays so small a part in primitive Shintoism; if we except the fact that this element is implicit in the cult of Emperors and Heroes and, in a more general way, in the cult of ancestors, the perspective of Shintō resembles that of the American Indians inasmuch as it lays stress upon present virtues rather than on the future of these virtues; their fruits are in fact included in the virtues themselves and guaranteed by them, the life beyond being strictly the effect of a man's values while yet on this earth; he who has grasped the cause will also grasp the effect. This perspective doubtless is closely related to the warrior tradition where words are of but little account and where the act, as a decisive affirmation of the immortal person, seems almost sufficient unto itself.

The same thing might be expressed otherwise by saying that Shintoists are free to ignore the beyond, as the case may be, provided they do not ignore either God or their own redemptive duties; just as contrariwise Monotheists can ignore the multitude of universes, and therefore also the 'extent' of the Round of Existence, Samsāra, that is to say the existence of extra-human worlds and the pre-adamic and post-apocalyptic cycles, provided they know all that relates to the human eschatology: if the reproach levelled by Monotheists at the Shinto-Shamanists is justified, the reproach levelled by Hindus and Buddhists at the Monotheists will be so likewise, and if this latter reproach is unfair, then the former one will not be any less unfair. In each case one must, however, pay due heed to such positive factors as make up for the respective ignorance shown.

In a comparable order of ideas the parsimony of the Shintō tradition in respect of moral precepts has also attracted notice: in this connexion we will quote the eighteenth century commentator Motoori: 'To know that there is no way to be followed is to know and follow the Way of the Gods',[1] that is to say to follow Shintō. The foundation of the virtues here is a consciousness of purity and impurity, of sincerity and insincerity, a consciousness that is readily related to the idea of 'honour'; it should also be added that life consists, very largely, of a series of somewhat similar situations, hence the ideas and practices found in Shintoism engender ways of acting that are practically the equivalent of moral precepts even though not given that form; this is all the more true in practice since these ways of acting have become ingrained in the habits of the collectivity.

All things considered, rather than be required to submit himself to a set of precepts, a man would do better to remain anchored in his state of original perfection, a statement that brings us back to the cult of ancestors: a man should not see, in his forebears or even in his immediate parents, anything but what is perfect; when it is said of a deceased person that he has become *kami* this means that he has rejoined his celestial prototype, of which he himself had been, down in this world, the manifestation, doubtless a precarious one but nevertheless real.

On the other hand, venerable men after their death bequeath to us a psychic element that is able to fix itself in a determinate place, most often in connexion with their bodily remains; the survivors offer worship, not only to the immortal and deified ancestor, but also to that tangible 'influence' (his *barakah* as Muslims would say) which subsists here below for their enlightenment and for their subsequent protection. The cult of relics has a similar meaning.

It is worth stressing the point that Shintoism sees in man, before all else, his global personality, innate virtue, of which human actions are possible but often only approximate mani-

---

[1] 'The way that one can follow is not the true Way,' says the *Tao-Te-King;* that is to say, action cannot lead to Actionlessness (*wu-wei*) nor thought alone to Knowledge. To cite a Christian parallel: according to the *Philokalia* 'the soul is righteous when its science remains in the state that is natural to it . . . When we remain as we were created, we are in a state of virtue.'

festations by reason of the gap between an act and its intention. The quality of the personal substance is supposed to have the power to neutralize imperfect or erroneous actions, though evidently it could also be argued that bad actions compromise the personality, which is equally true: both views are legitimate, but each is opportune for the mentality it reflects and to which it appeals. In a certain sense, the Shintoist morality has two poles, namely 'caste', which has to be maintained, and the purificatory and other prescriptions, which have to be obeyed; caste, divine origin, essentially implies a 'solar' perfection, comparable to that sacred Mirror which is like the very image of Shintō and which will be described later.

There are ways of acting, feeling and thinking that are shared by all Japanese – at least in so far as they remain true to themselves – and which perhaps derive as much from the warrior code of Bushidō and from a Confucianist inspiration as from pure Shintō: viewed from outside, this is a matter of a complex and subtle civility, but in a more interior sense this unwritten law can go further and canalize the soul after the manner of a *karma-yoga* or an *islam*. The Shintoist ethic, which claims for the Yamato race the attribute 'divine', perhaps is essentially a *style of action;* it is in fact possible to conceive a perspective where style would count before contents whereof it would largely neutralize the imperfections, since a noble form necessarily opposes itself to base actions: the archaic notion of a salvation reserved for a caste can be explained in these terms. Under the rather special conditions here being considered it is not the caste, properly speaking, that constitutes an *élite*, but rather the *élite* which constitutes the caste; that is to say, emphasis is laid on quality itself rather than on its framework. Quality, for its part, is guaranteed and controlled by discipline and the manner of living; here heredity is only a providential factor.

*

The Tennō or Celestial Monarch[1] is like the incarnation of Shintō; he is descended through his ancestor Jimmu Tennō

[1] Though *Tennō* is the official title of the Emperor, his poetical appelation of *Mikado* ('Sublime Gate') is more familiar to Europeans.

from Amaterasu-Omikami, the solar Goddess, she herself being
the issue of the divine Couple Izanagi and Izanami. Amaterasu-
Omikami, the 'great Divinity of the shining Sky', is also named
Ohirumemuchi-no-Kami, 'She who possesses the great Sun'
and she corresponds to the universal and creative Intellect, to
the luminous and merciful Centre of the cosmos, therefore to
what the Hindu doctrine denotes by *Buddhi* and the Islamic
doctrine by *Er-Ruh*, Spirit; and just as Buddhi under its aspect
of Vishnu incarnates itself in human Avatāras such as Rama
and Krishna, so also does Amaterasu engender Jimmu Tennō,
founder and first Emperor of Japan.[1] As for the divine Couple,
this is no other than the syzygy Purusha – Prakriti of the
Hindu cosmology; 'seven divine generations' are said to have
preceded the divine Couple, evidently representing possibilities
that inhere in Being but in principial and therefore simultaneous
mode and without actually being called forth into manifestation.

We know that in Hinduism Purusha and Prakriti are the
creative polarizations – 'masculine' and feminine' – of Being,
Ishvara, who himself is the auto-determination of Beyond-
Being, Brahma. In Shintō the supreme Principle is Ame-no-
Minakanushi-no-Kami, the 'divine Lord of the Centre of the
Heavens', of whom it is said that He 'hath engendered Himself'
and that He 'hath neither parents nor spouse nor children';
His 'non-acting' is reminiscent of the *wu-wei* of Taoism. Some-
times He is apparently replaced by Kuni-Tokotachi-no-Mikoto,
'Eternal divine earthly Being', which doubtless refers to Being
properly so-called and which thus would correspond to Ishvara
Himself; here the word 'earthly' seems to be a reference to
Existence or productive power, 'earth' being often used, in the
mythological languages, as a synonym of 'manifestation'.[2]

Just as the Couple Purusha-Prakriti, in the Hindu symbolism,
gives rise to Brahmā, Vishnu, Shiva, Saraswatī, Lakshmī,
Parvatī and by extension or sub-division to other celestial

[1] Jimmu Tennō founded the Empire in 660 B.C. that is to say about the time
of the Buddha, Lao-Tse and Confucius.

[2] There is one group of Shintoists, known as the Konkō school, who worship
Tenchi-Kame-no-Kami, 'the Divinity who embraces Heaven and Earth', that
is to say *Ātmā*, the Divine Self, who contains all things. For the Kurozumi
school, God is 'sincerity', or to be more accurate he is the infinite Light of which
this virtue is the human projection.

aspects or angelic functions and lastly to the whole world, so also Izanami gives birth to various refractions of the cosmic Light, namely Earth represented by the Japanese islands and the gods of Nature. As for Izanagi, he by himself alone engenders the 'Three noble Children' who are: the solar Amaterasu-Omikami, who is gentle and loving and who reigns over the high celestial spheres: Tsukiyomi-no-Mikoto, Divinity of the Moon, who reigns over the kingdom of night: and Susano-wo-no-Mikoto, Divinity of the Tempest, who reigns over the sea and earth. According to other sources the above three divinities are procreated by the divine Couple, Izanagi-Izanami; they correspond to the cosmic constituents referred to in the Hindu doctrine as *sattva*, *rajas*, *tamas*, the luminous (or ascendent), the calorific (expansive) and the darkening (compressive) principle respectively, which they represent, however, in principial or 'archangelic' mode, on the model of the Hindu *Trimūrti*.

If the above-mentioned divinities be taken as emanating from Izanagi alone – in Hindu parlance from Purusha – this is by reason of the pre-eminent distinction that exists, in the Cosmos, between its quasi-divine or 'archangelic' centre and the periphery, of which the extreme limit, for our world, will be Matter; thus also, in the human being, Intellect is distinguished from 'body-and-soul' that forms the ego. In other words, the cosmic Centre, which is supra-formal, is attributed to Izanagi ('the male who invites' = Purusha) and the world of form to Izanami ('the female who invites' = Prakriti) conjointly with Izanagi: like the relationship 'principle-manifestation', the relationship 'centre-periphery' or plane of manifestation is equivalent to the complementary opposition 'virility-femininity', which goes to explain the intention behind the Shintoist symbolism we are discussing.

We have seen that the divine Couple engenders the Japanese isles, which constitute a reduced image of the Universe; all Nature with its mountains, water, fauna and flora, together with the human race – represented by the Japanese people – is the work of the divine Couple. Therefore the divine origin of Japan coincides, symbolically speaking, with that of the World, in much the same way as the end of Jerusalem, in Christ's prophecies, coincides with the end of the world; that which Jimmu Tennō, 'superhuman man', brought to the Japanese is not simply a divine origin in the order of temporal succession, but also a consciousness of this divine origin which is proper to all men and the forgetfulness of which entails the loss of all human virtues and rights; it is perfectly natural that Japan, as being the 'scene' of the Shintoic Revelation, should be, for the latter, its world centre, for such is, *mutatis mutandis*, the point of view of every traditional perspective: that 'place' is 'centre' where God has manifested Himself. Hence it will be easy to understand that an objection based on the fact that the population of Japan – with the exception of the Ainus – arrived in the times called 'prehistoric' from Korea, Southern China and the Malay Archipelago and therefore must have been in existence prior to Jimmu Tennō is without importance in this context, granted that the population of the Japanese islands, before the founding of the Empire, was still undergoing a process of 'chaotic elaboration'. Jimmu Tennō united the tribes and by 'divine command' made of the human *materia* thus providentially assembled within the same country a 'mirror' of humanity and of the Universe: he was, in a direct sense a 'son of the Solar Goddess' because, being 'born of Spirit', he was 'without origin or end'.

*

Like all other mythologies, that of Shintō includes features which at first sight may seem bewildering but which are profoundly symbolical: thus it is a bird – a wagtail – that taught copulation to the divine Pair; here the bird stands for the demiurgic and deifugal tendency and retraces, in the cosmogonic order, the biblical mystery of the serpent. Concerning the strange features associated with the Shintoist cosmogony, perhaps the most apt commentary is that of Motoori Norinaga (eighteenth century) when he said: 'Who would have invented so ridiculous a story, were it not true?' To which he adds that human intelligence, being limited, is unable to understand the actions of the Gods. Similarly Ānanda K. Coomaraswamy has written: 'For so long as men still understood the true nature of their myths they were not shocked by their "immorality". The myths are never, in fact, immoral but, like every other form of theory (vision), amoral. . . . The content of the myths is intellectual rather than moral . . . and whosoever deprecates the hero's "morals" has already misconceived the genus'.[1]

To return to the Shintō myth, it is further related that Izanami, after giving birth to the last of her sons Homusubi, God of Fire, succumbed to her burns and had to go down into hell, of which she became the goddess. In fact, the cosmic Substance does also have a darksome aspect of chaos and unintelligibility, which shows itself as soon as one comes to consider the rupture of equilibrium brought about by the actualization and differentiation of the cosmic tendencies, but solely at their own level: to speak in Hindu terms, although Prakriti always remains virginal on her own principial plane, she appears to be modified on the relatively illusory plane of her productions, where the appearance of the principle fire-cum-light carries with it the principles of passion and obscurity – passion by 'individuation' and obscurity by 'inversion' – which amounts, in Christian symbolism, to the distinction between Lucifer and Satan; the confines of existential totality seem to be submerged in a kind of nothingness that never is quite reached.

The same truth is expressed by the myth of the descent of Izanagi into hell: Izanami, who has already tasted the infernal food, is unwilling to accompany her spouse back to the upper air; however she consents to submit the question to the sub-terranean gods, but on condition that Izanagi does not look inside her house; after a long wait, however, he loses patience, peeps through the window and catches sight of the festering corpse of Izanami who, for her part, feeling that she has been 'slighted' rushes out in pursuit of Izanagi, assisted by the denizens of hell;[2] but he escapes from the world of darkness and blocks up the entrance with a huge boulder and thus the two partners are separated; then Izanagi, after washing in the river,

---

[1] *On the loathly Bride* (in *Speculum*, October 1945).

[1] That is to say Matter, though 'divine' inasmuch as it forms bodily creatures, nonetheless includes an aspect of hostility to the Spirit. The material world, multiple and impure by reason of life itself, is none other than the 'sub-terranean' and 'slighted' body of Izanami, that body of which the 'protoform' is ever dwelling in its incorruptible virginity.

gives birth to Amaterasu, Tsukiyomi and Susano-wo. This descent into hell is reminiscent not only of the myth of Orpheus and Eurydice but also of the medieval legend of Raimondin and Melusine and it also recalls, by certain of its details, the Bible account of the fall of Adam and Eve; in all these myths we see *natura naturans* being transmuted into *natura naturata* or revealing herself under the latter aspect; the Spouse of the creative Spirit loses her divine nature, is recognized by the Spirit as non-divine and thus becomes separated from him. But as this drama is only played on the ambiguous plane of Existence, the Spouse remains intact *in divinis*, hence the union of Eurydice and Orpheus in the Elysian fields and the final reuniting of the lovers of Lusignan.[1]

Mention should also be made of the fact that the divine Couple of Shintō gave birth to two abortions, a 'leech' and an 'islet of foam', this, because Izanami, when she met Izanagi, was the first to speak; on the occasion of their second meeting it was Izanagi who spoke first, and then they gave birth to Japan, that is to say the terrestrial world. Here again can be seen a certain parallel with the sin of Adam and Eve; what the Japanese myth wishes to bring out is that initiative for evil or initiative in favour of the deifugal tendency comes from the 'female' element, which 'seduces', whereas creation as such – the positive content of existence and not the existential separation – emanates from the 'male' element. Eve, who is of earth, gets Adam to believe that she is formed of heavenly substance, which is true as regards her essence, but not so as regards her 'accidents'; here there is a confusing of planes, not an error affecting the essential reality.

Izanami dies while giving birth to Kagotsuchi, the 'radiant one', also named Homusubi, 'He who engenders the fire': if one may hazard an explanation, it would seem that the devouring Fire causes to appear, in regard to the Substance it feeds on,

---

[1] In the ancient Egyptian mythology, Osiris, slain by Seth and then cut in pieces to fertilize the earth, springs from the same symbolism: in both cases, the immolated Divinities prefigure death, through the gates of which all living beings needs must pass. Again in Islam, it is said that after sinning Eve lost her beauty and was parted from Adam for five centuries. Adam forgot Eve and did penance but, as in the myths described above, the two primordial parents finally met again; they were reunited on Mount Arafat.

the latter's mortal character and thus it is by Fire that the contrast between *natura naturans* and *natura naturata* is as if unveiled; in the Fire, the divine Spirit is embodied inasmuch as it is opposable to Substance or matter, which is the same as saying that there is analogy between the birth of Fire – mortal for the Mother – and the impatience of the Husband, as expressed in his glance that provoked the separation. Plainly here it is only a question of cosmic principles, of which the corporeal elements apparent to the senses are the most 'external' manifestations; it is true, however, that earth , in all her impotence and impurity, corresponds in one sense to the infernal body of Izanami and that the glance of Izanagi is like the discernment between cosmic Substance and this 'coagulation-limit'.

Herein one can also recognize an analogy with the first glance of Adam and Eve following their sin, whereby their own nakedness was revealed to them; it marks the passage from a perspective that is 'interior', principial, synthetic and unitive to one that is 'exterior', contingent, analytical and separative; what is seen is no longer the unity of essence, the immutable Principle, but the existential plane, contingent manifestation.

In the Shintoist myth Izanami, humiliated, says in effect to her spouse: 'You have beheld my state; now I shall behold your state in my turn'. Whereupon Izanagi is likewise humiliated and answers 'Our kinship is broken'; the exact nature of his humiliation is not made clear. To sum up the lesson of this whole story: the divine Wife died because there was born the Fire that burns up the cosmic veils, those that conceal from the eyes of the divine Husband the existential planes or contingent degrees, the reflection in contingency, that is to say; and as for him – thinking to see universal Substance ever beautiful and virgin he suddenly perceives earthly matter, which is her most inferior reflection or 'dead-point'. Fire, in fact, causes a passage, at least in a symbolical sense, from one degree of reality to another; that which *a priori* appears as a heavenly thing is revealed, once Fire has consumed it, as wretched matter; a certain tree that formerly might have been regarded as of paradise and immortal is reduced to a worthless heap of ashes; from having been a divine aspect, it is now but dust. Let it be said, in addition, that the 'vertical' perspective of all mythologies, as also the mentality of the more or less primordial men to whom mythologies address themselves, clearly distinguishes the Fire-principle from physical fire, but it does not make an 'essential' distinction between the two; this is the most important point to be noted concerning all phenomena of the genus *kami*. On the other hand, whenever one has to do with stories of this kind, one must never forget that what in the story is presented as a series of events really represents a principial situation, therefore one pertaining to the Changeless.

*

No less significant is the myth telling about the captivity of the Sun in the Cavern: the opposition, on a cosmic scale, between Knowledge and Passion is presented as a struggle between Sun and Tempest, Amaterasu-Omikami and her brother Susano-wo-no-Mikoto. In order to avoid the violence of her brother, the solar Goddess hides herself in the celestial Cavern, causing a total obscuration of all the regions of the Universe; then the 'eight hundred myriads of Gods' – refractions of the intelligible Light now cut off from their divine Source and so to speak deprived of life – cause Amaterasu to come forth by the play of a mirror as symbolized by the solar disc. As an additional lure there was the cock's crow, the dancing of the goddess Uzume uncovering her body and the laughter of the gods; now there is an evident symbolical connexion between cock-crow and the dawn, between the uncovering of the secrets of a lovely body and the sun's coming forth from the darkness, and lastly between the laughter that sets free and the sudden flashing of the new-born day. Some have thought they recognized in the above-mentioned dance a symbol of fertilization; moreover, the goddess danced on an inverted tub and made it resound by striking it with her lance, which has been interpreted as a sexual symbolism. Uzume while dancing was affected by a 'divine possession': this is the prototype of the Kagura, the sacred dance of the great feasts.

The mirror, which is none other than the Intelligence governing the sensible world (= *Virāj* of the Hindu cosmology) 'sucks up' the Light towards the cosmic labyrinth of which the channels (receptacles of light like the mirror) precisely are identified with the 'myriads of Gods'. As in the case of the mirror, it is necessary to distinguish between an aspect of 'receptivity' and an aspect of 'luminosity', according to whether one is looking 'downwards' or 'upwards'; in relation to the initial Light, to Amaterasu, the 'solar mirror' and 'the Gods' are receptacles, but in relation to the spheres which they respectively illumine, they themselves are light. In the same myth, Susano-wo is banished to the earth, which indicates the final victory of 'the Sun' over 'the Tempest' or, to be more precise, of Knowledge over the passionate element; but the latter in its capacity of 'productive energy' is still necessary to the cosmic economy, and that is why Susano-wo had earthly issue, though without losing his celestial dignity; nonetheless he is, in a sense, the first sinner.

To pursue these cosmological analogies somewhat further: as the solar mirror corresponds to Virāj, Amaterasu-Omikami will in her turn correspond to Hiranyagarbha, the 'golden embryo' whence the world proceeds; Jimmu Tennō will then be – always speaking in Hindu terms – equivalent to Manu the primordial lawgiver, at least on the scale of the Japanese Universe. In the temple of Ise, the Holy of Holies of Shintoism, they have preserved a replica of, or substitute for, the octagonal mirror that fetched Amaterasu out of the Cavern; this earthly mirror – which of necessity is not the work of human hands – is the seat of the 'Real Presence' of the Divinity, which thus is present at the rites and listens to the prayers.

'According to the ancient tradition, when Ninigi-no-Mikoto descended from the "Plain of Heaven" (*Takama-ga-Hana*) to the summit of mount Takachiho in the province of Hiuga in order to assume sway over the lower world (Japan), his grandmother the Sun Goddess presented him with a sacred mirror with instruction to keep it always at his side, in the living-room of his palace; whenever he looked into it, he was to remember he was seeing the goddess herself as ever present within. It is said that this custom was solemnly observed by all the succeeding Emperors down to the time of the Emperor Sujin at the beginning of the first century B.C., but that Sujin, overawed at the thought of such close proximity to so sacred an object and fearing that calamity might befall him and his realm, had a shrine built for it in the village of Kasanui in the province of Yamato and assigned the care of it to his virgin daughter Toyosuki Irihime. This was then the beginning of an age marked by a distinct separation between the human and the divine. About the beginning of the Christian era the sacred emblem was transferred to the province of Ise, where the great shrine has remained ever since'.[1]

One more detail of the mytho-cosmology of Shintō needs to be mentioned here: plants sprang from the manifold hairs of Susano-wo-no-Mikoto; or again, living creatures issued from the corpse of the Goddess of Sustenance, Ukemochi. Here one cannot help being reminded of similar myths to be found in the Rigvēda and the Mundaka-Upanishad: the world springs from the sacrifice of Purusha, of whom the immolated portions become creatures in their diversity as well as the human castes as such; however – and this is a most important point metaphysically – it is only 'one quarter' of Purusha that is thus fragmented, while the other 'three quarters' remain unaffected in the immutability of the Principle.

In the 'divine age' earth was still joined to Heaven by the bridge *Ama-no-Hashidate*; this bridge collapsed while the Gods were asleep. This sleep marks a kind of 'divine absence', therefore a deprivation of Grace on earth; it is, however, important to remember that this absence could only be a 'concordant reaction' or karmic answer to 'an absence' on the part of men in relation to Heaven. This is a spiritual truth that admits of no gainsaying.

*

The complexity of the world's mythologies, their enigmas and apparent incoherencies, are explainable not only by differences of perspective to which every science – and 'sacred science' most of all – is liable, but also by a diversity in levels of reality: an identical principle can be considered at one and the same time in different modes and at different degrees, so

[1] Quoted from *Honen the Buddhist Saint* by Ringaku Ishizuka and Harper Havelock Coates, Kyoto, 1949.

much so that a certain fluctuation is unavoidable as between viewpoints and aspects, reflecting differences of local tradition; it is as if 'vertical' realities, intersected by 'horizontal' planes, were oscillating between Heaven and earth, and it is not without good reason that it could be said of ancient Japan that here 'the notions of god and priest were mingled together'. If the Gods do not seem to have been omniscient, if, for example, they put questions to human diviners, this is for the same reason as, according to the Koran, the Angels had to learn the names of all things from Adam: it goes with the fact that Man, as a 'central' being, is situated at the foot of the 'vertical axis' uniting earth to Heaven, whereas the Angels, though superior to man as regards their existential level, are nevertheless situated in the 'spiroidal periphery' of the cosmos, excepting the Archangels, who occupy the degree of universal Intellect, but whose secondary personifications precisely are what constitute the ordinary angels; from which it follows that 'a god' can be envisaged at three degrees, angelic, archangelic and divine. This type of complexity will make it plain why a mythology appears under a form that is more or less discontinous or disparate, after the manner of a mosaic and not under the form of a homogeneous enunciation, also why it is necessarily accompanied by an oral or written commentary; moreover the inspired commentators, legitimate by reason of their orthodoxy, intervene, not in order to add, over and above the sacred symbolism, some conjectural interpretations of their own contriving, but on the contrary in order to draw out of those symbols the lights enshrined therein since the beginning. In the tradition which it is their mission to preserve through rendering it intelligible according to the varying needs of the times, that which at first sight might appear abstruse is but the sign of the inexhaustible potential of Revelation.

One must avoid, in this realm, the convenient but useless hypothesis of 'borrowings'; for example, the fact that the left eye of Izanagi gave birth to the Sun and the right eye to the Moon – to Amaterasu and Tsukiyomi respectively – in no wise authorises one to suppose that this myth has been copied from some Chinese myth that happens to resemble it, for the analogy between eyes and heavenly bodies is deeply rooted in the nature of things and is to be found in the most diverse traditions. Physiognomists are not unaware that the right eye expresses the future and the left eye the past, and the relation of the sun to the future and the moon to the past is perfectly plausible; nor is it without reason that the moon has been assimilated to 'cosmic memory'. If in the Japanese myth it is the left eye, contrary to expectation, that gives birth to the Sun, this is because here the Sun is envisaged, just as in the Germanic languages, under an aspect of femininity, of which it will then represent, not its passive and fragmentary side, but on the contrary its active or maternal side: the Sun possesses fecundity, he is active in 'creating' children, whereas the Moon – male according to a matriarchal perspective – is 'sterile' in the sense that it knows not maternity, which alone is a 'beaming forth'; the lunar male wanes in fruitless solitude, obtaining no expansion except thanks to Woman who in giving him joy confers upon him, as it were, a life-giving light. In this manner of viewing things it is the past that appears 'real' or 'better', exactly as happens in ancestor-worship or in the idea of 'tradition' generally and for the same reasons: the future is unreality, uncertainty, that which, humanly speaking, has not been and is able not to be; in any case the future is that which cannot be except as a result of the past; the past is identified with the origin – hence also with the timeless; and the future, inasmuch as it is beatitude or deliverance, is the return to the origin, and therefore also to Eternity.

*

An alternative version of the myth of Izanagi and Izanami represents the three Divinities – Amaterasu, Tsukiyomi and Susano-wo – as being born before Homusubi, therefore prior to the descent of Izanami into the 'Land of Darkness'; in that case, the three Divinities do not spring from Izanagi alone but are the product of the divine Couple; the two perspectives are only separated by a matter of emphasis or specification, with the one considering the common act of the ontological poles and the other stressing the special relation existing between the male Principle and the cosmic Centre – constituted by the three Divinities – as was explained above.

On the other hand, we have also seen that the death of Izanami prefigures the death of every creature; as the story goes, it is Izanami who causes beings to die in order to avenge the 'slight' inflicted on herself by Izanagi while he, for his part, is for ever recreating life in order to re-establish a balance. The breach – a relative and illusory breach, however – between the divine Husband and Wife manifests itself consequently as a war between life and death, the latter coming from *natura naturata* or *materia secunda*, that is to say from the material coagulation of the macrocosmic Substance, while life is always arising afresh from the creative Principle, or rather from its male and 'vertical' aspect. And this again leads us back to the biblical myth according to which it is by woman that death has come into the world; the Holy Virgin, who overcomes death, is like a personification of the celestial and non-materialized aspect of universal Substance, which always remains virgin in respect to her own productions.

At the time of the break between the divine Pair, the Wife said to the Husband: 'Each day I shall cause a thousand of your people to die in your kingdom'; to which Izanagi replied: 'And I shall give birth every day to one thousand five hundred people', which expresses symbolically the disproportion between death and life. Howbeit, it is not only death and life that arose out of this breach, but also darkness and light, war and peace and all the remaining contrasts of the cosmos; it is also said that at the moment when Izanagi returned from hell and washed off his defilements, the infernal mud produced Yaso-Maga-Tsu-Hi, the genius of multiple calamities who was followed immediately by Kamu-Nahobi, the genius of repair. It is interesting to note the fact that the Singhalese recognize a similar destructive genius, going by the name of Maha-Kola-Sanni-Yaksaya, the demon of great diseases, whose every head stands for a different evil. In the Greek mythology Pandora plays at the same time the part of Yaso-Maga-Tsu-Hi and Izanami, therefore also the part of Eve.

Yet another difference of perspective worth pointing out is as follows: it was said before that the supreme Principle is Ame-no-Minakanushi-no-Kami, the 'divine Lord of the Centre of the Heavens', and that this divine Name is sometimes replaced by that of Kuni-Tokotachi-no-Mikoto, 'Eternal divine terrestrial Being' or 'He who eternally stands over the world'; now some other interpretations see in these two one divinity only, or again, they add to them yet more divinities, calling this whole assemblage *Daigenshin*, the 'Great divine Origin'; the latter in its turn is identified with Amaterasu-Omikami, the solar Goddess, who thus assumes (as in the case of Amida in Pure Land Buddhism) the part of supreme Divinity. This example will give an idea of the complexity of mythologies in general and of Shintō in particular.

Before concluding this section it is well to consider yet another aspect of the cosmogonic myth: it is said that the divine Couple, standing on the 'floating bridge of the Sky' (the rainbow) stirred the sea with their celestial lance enriched with precious stones; a drop of sea water that fell from the lance became the island Onokoro (= 'Self-coagulated'), and it was there that the Pair established themselves before proceeding to the creation of beings. The reader hardly needs reminding that in traditional lore throughout the world the rainbow symbolizes the meeting of Heaven and Earth; one has only to think of the 'rainbow-bridge' into Valhalla in the Nordic tradition and the symbolism of Iris in the Hellenic myths. As for the lance, this makes one think of the phallic symbolism under its many forms, as for example the 'Reed-pen' and 'Ink' of the Islamic doctrine, and still more of the 'vertical axis' of Purusha in the Hindu doctrine which by its crossing with the 'horizontal axis' of Prakriti occasions the creative effusion. The sea, in the Shintoist myth, is none other than the sum total of possibilities of manifestation and thus it is identifiable with the 'Lower Waters' of the Hebraic doctrine;[1] if it be Susano-wo, God of the Storm, who governs 'the sea', this is precisely because of the 'passionate' character of the demiurgic movement.[2] On the

[1] The 'Upper Waters' in that tradition indicate the prototype of those possiblities *in divinis*, that is to say the infinite Beatitude.

[2] On the subject of the Storm-God, let it be added that, exiled on earth, he engendered 'evil spirits'; his sister Amaterasu despatched her celestial armies against them and their allies (or she sent armies helped by Heaven) and after the victory she established the imperial dynasty still reigning over Japan. The descendants of Susano-wo are purely passionate creatures, violent and harmful therefore, but necessary for the sake of cosmic equilibrium; in this sense they

other hand, if the primordial chaos is compared, in Shintō, to an 'ocean of oil', this is because of the 'weight' and 'warmth' of that substance, 'weight' being a reference to existential 'solidification' and 'warmth' to the 'passional' character we have just alluded to.

---

are 'of divine origin'. They correspond, not to demons strictly speaking, but to the 'giants' and 'titans' of European mythologies, as also to the inhabitants of Asura-Loka in the Buddhist diagram of the Round of Existence, Samsāra. The demoniac order is 'subterranean' and not 'marine' like that of the Storm-god.

CHAPTER XIII

THE NOBLE VIRTUES: SOME LESSONS OF SHINTŌ

I⊤ was said before that the Tennō is like an incarnation of Shintō from the fact that he is descended, through Jimmu Tennō, Founder of the Empire, from the solar Goddess Amaterasu-Omikami; it now remains for us to mention the spiritual prerogatives implied in this origin and function. One can, by analogy, form some opinion of these prerogatives by referring to the rather similar case of the Sherifs in Islam – the descendants of the Prophet – who enjoy a privileged situation in a human and even an eschatological sense: none of them will go to hell, for God has pardoned them from beforehand thanks to the *barakah* (spiritual influence) attaching to the blood of Muhammad; one has to accept their eventual shortcomings as one accepts divine decrees, with patience and if possible even with gratitude; their blessing is beneficial, their curse brings ill-luck; if they are pious, they have every chance of reaching sainthood. Such privileges, that are far from arbitrary (however surprising this may seem at first sight) are attached to every line that is of 'avatāric' origin, therefore also to the line of Jimmu Tennō who, for his part, incontestably had the quality of a 'Prophet'. From this it must be inferred that the divine character of the Tennō cannot be abolished either by legislation or even by the Emperor himself, whose individual wishes have no power over his hereditary nature or the virtualities that it comprises. The case of the Chinese Emperors seems to have been somewhat different: according to the traditional interpretation of their function it was exercised in virtue of a 'heavenly mandate', which might be withdrawn, as could also happen with the Emperors of Constantinople and the Califs of Islam.

It goes without saying that, as far as the individuals holding an office of avatāric ancestry is concerned, such as that of Sherif or Tennō, the principle of 'noblesse oblige' applies, thus requiring of them that they should if possible exemplify, not only passively but also consciously, those virtues of which their respective ancestors were like the incarnations.

The noble or imperial virtues, in Shintō, essentially are represented by the 'Three Treasures', namely the Mirror, Sword and Jewel; respectively these stand for truth, courage and compassion, or else wisdom, strength and charity; here the parallelism with Mahāyāna Buddhism is striking, where the same three preeminent virtues are personified by the celestial Bodhisattvas Manjusri (Wisdom), Avalokitēsvara (Compassion) and Vajrapani (Power). According to tradition the sacred Treasures in the beginning amounted to ten, namely the 'mirror of the open sea', the 'mirror of the shore', the 'sword of eight spans', the 'lifegiving jewel', the 'jewel of health and strength', the 'jewel that raises the dead', the 'jewel that keeps off evil from the ways' and the 'scarves of diverse powers'; all these were transferred from Heaven to earth. In the course of history many miracles are on record as having taken place thanks to the supernatural virtues of these treasures which have been compared, not without reason, to the Ark of the Covenant of the Jews.

The mirror is the most important symbol of Shintoism, so much so that it amounts to a substitute for an image of God; and similarly it is sincerity – closely related to the element 'truth' – that here ranks as the cardinal virtue. One could also speak of 'purity' in the same sense: at the origins, physical cleanliness, now become a characteristic feature of the Japanese people, coincided with mental and moral purity; the lustral water has a quasi-sacramental quality, as it likewise possesses in other religions where ritual ablutions play a part. As for sincerity, this is far from reducible to a relatively external moral rectitude; its connection with truth, on the one hand, and with the symbolism of the mirror, on the other, indicates that its scope is much greater, being calculated to bring the whole being back to the ontological source of man's sense of truth; the human soul is made in order to identify itself with the divine Mirror, which is at the same time radiant and relentless like the sun.

The mirror, as we have seen, takes the place of an image of God; Shintoism indeed has an 'iconoclastic' side that relates it, in this one respect, to the Jewish and Islamic religions; nevertheless, the absence of images in Shintoism has motives behind it that differ from those animating the Semitic Monotheism. In point of fact the Shintō perspective is nearer to that of the Red Indians who do not try to depict the Great Spirit either; this amounts to saying that this perspective is centred on Nature regarded in her virginity and divinity, and this is an attitude that has nothing to do with the Semitic fear of idolatry, as is proved moreover by the eventual introduction into Japan of Buddhist images and especially by the unsurpassable quality of Buddhist art in that country. Rather is it a case of seeing the Divinity through the phenomena of Nature, including animals, in such a light as to render the use of other sacred images superfluous.

Shintoist sanctuaries are virtually empty; they merely contain, in a Holy of Holies inaccessible to visitors, the mirror and the sword. Popular portrayals of Shintō divinities do not derive from a sacred Canon although they are obviously traditional in style.

The foregoing remarks warrant a digression: Jews and Muslims usually believe that the biblical and koranic interdiction of 'idols' representing God refers to Christian, Hindu and Buddhist sacred images; but this view springs from a misunderstanding regarding the nature and purpose of the latter: one might express the difference of the two things by specifying that when God said to Moses 'Thou shalt not make graven images' He did not say 'I shall make no images': properly sacred images, in the traditions where they belong, are inspired and therefore made by God, not man. On the other hand, Greco-Roman images of the 'classical' period as also the naturalistic Christian images of later times, modelled on their style, plainly fall under the divine prohibition as being the work of human minds and hands and nothing besides.

In the West, some people think they can discern idolatry not only in Buddhism but even in Shintō and in the latter case they will speak of stone-worship, water-worship or zoolatry etc. not forgetting the misunderstood cult of the Mirror. Now idolatry consists essentially in a reduction of the content of a symbol to the image itself, in isolation from any metaphysical background; consequently, idolatry by definition excludes all consciousness of symbolism. What characterizes Buddhism, as also Hinduism and every other comparable doctrine, is precisely this, namely that it likes to express – as for instance in its theory of *upāyas*, spiritual means – its consciousness of the 'mythological' character attaching to all formal data; and that is also why it hardly troubles to give its symbols any semblance of historicity, indeed quite the contrary; it sets out to awaken a presentiment of the great rending of the veil that is to come and it tries to suggest from beforehand that facts themselves are nothing but 'emptiness'.

Some people think they are able to make Shintō square with contemporary thought by stressing its character of a 'natural religion': if they wished to convey by this phrase that Shintō is anchored in the symbolism as also in the metaphysical transparence of nature, they would be right; but as the intention is to oppose it to 'supernatural religion' the phrase in question becomes meaningless and quite unjustifiable. To speak of a 'natural religion' is a contradiction in terms just as it is a pleonasm to speak of a 'supernatural religion'. A religion either is or is not; to describe it as being purely 'natural' and 'human' amounts to saying that it is valueless, devoid of authority or of any real efficacy. Moreover, since religion is superhuman by definition it cannot 'evolve' and its historical deployment does not add to it any fresh or essential quality. It is true that, humanly speaking, the Revelations in order to become civilizations require that certain ideas and patterns of behaviour should obtain a progressive hold upon the collectivity, just as traditions requiring to become separated from pre-existing civilizations, as has been the case with Buddhism and Christianity, have need of certain gropings and a period of elaboration in order to become altogether conscious of themselves; but all this concerns traditions only in so far as they are formal and collective phenomena and not as spiritual realities that concern individual man.

That the properly esoteric 'dimension' of Shintō was provided by the Mahāyāna is highly probable, and this would indeed confer added meaning on the symbolism of these two associated traditions; one might then say, perhaps, that Shintō corresponds approximately to the 'Lesser Mysteries' of Western Antiquity, while the Mahāyāna represents the 'Greater Mysteries', those that lead beyond the 'current of forms'. It would however be surprising if Shintō did not also include an esotericism of its own, as in fact it does; yet it would seem that the arrival of the Buddhist esotericism was providential, that is to say that it answered to a profound need of the Japanese soul: evidence for this is the emergence, in Japan, of a number of original Buddhist schools, not to mention the surpassing quality of Japanese Buddhist art to which reference has often been made in these pages.

*

The question may now fairly be put whether Shintō, apart from having given form to the life of the Japanese, has anything particular to offer to the rest of mankind; consideration of this question will provide a fitting conclusion to the present essay.

After the disaster of 1945 some voices made themselves heard in the sense of trying to lay at the door of Shintō the blame for the excesses of the Japanese nationalists – and here let us not forget that 'nationalism' is a modern Western notion, imported into Japan together with many other things; in imputing these things to the tradition that had protected Japan ever since the founding of the Empire, for over two thousand years therefore, these would-be critics showed very little imagination, otherwise they would have asked themselves whether there might not exist other ascertainable causes for a calamity dating from such a recent past! In the nineteenth century some people were inclined to level similar reproaches at Buddhism, without pausing to consider whether the material force of the West and its imposition on Japan might not after all be the result of a spiritual aberration and consequently likely to prove a two-edged weapon in the long run. Unfortunately the apparently unlimited power of the Europeans was taken at that time for a criterion of truth in all Oriental countries one after the other, and this, in spite of many local attempts at resistance. It may well be, therefore, that the true lessons of 1945 are diametrically opposite to the ones usually drawn from those events; a re-reading of the evidence with this possibility in mind might lead to some salutary self-questioning on the part of those who still remain so infatuated with the modern Western civilization and what it has brought them, in which 1945, both in its causes and its effects, must logically be included.

To return to Shintō and its positive contribution to the common store of mankind: it strikes us first of all by its sensible manifestations, by the truly fascinating quality of its art and its rites and, in a more general sense, by the pure, fresh, primordial something that it exhales. Japanese craftsmanship, quite apart from its Chinese or Buddhist inheritance, is distinguished by an exquisite simplicity and a kind of sober refinement allowing one to guess all that the Japanese soul contains of precious gifts, namely an innate feeling for Nature and the natural – a feeling which allows a craftsman in Japan to create a masterpiece out of a handful of grass – coupled with the love of beauty, self-mastery, courtesy and heroism.

To the question as to how it was possible for the most artistic people on earth to have adopted with eagerness the errors and hideousness of the industrialized West one may perhaps find an answer by putting another question, namely how it was possible for the European Middle Ages, already in possession of a perfect art, to perpetrate a similar betrayal at the time of the Renaissance and in defiance of the same Christian morality on which this neo-paganism was making its frontal attack? Also how could 'Holy Russia', heir to Byzantine glories and housing a people second to none in piety, succumb to that same influence despite its own rooted dislike of the Latin West? The only possible explanation of such happenings is that tradition and sacred art come from Heaven and that their corruption comes from men. The success, in Japan as elsewhere, of the male attire of the West – an accoutrement at once puritan, revolutionary and industrialist – can be explained by the very fact that it expresses and suggests, with the insistence of a profession of faith, the fancied cosmic and eschatological 'extraterritoriality' of modern man; whereas all forms of traditional clothing without exception remain within the gearing of our final human ends, so to speak, whence their compatibility with the sacred.

Much praise has been given, and rightly so, to the qualities of Japanese woman-kind, but what is forgotten by those who proclaim her 'emancipation' is the fact of those traditional conditions that went into her forming. The sexes are not two races, the one tyrannical and the other tyrannized over; every woman has a father just as every man has a mother: the Japanese woman would not be what she is had she not inherited the qualities of strength, authority and discipline from innumerable fathers, just as Japanese man has benefitted, no less, from the gentleness, patience and self-sacrifice accumulated over centuries by his mothers. In quite a general way and outside any problem of the metaphysical and physiological differences of the sexes with their consequent inequalities, when people speak of 'freedom' they too easily forget that freedom only has value insofar as it allows of our realizing our spiritual destiny, conformably with our true nature. Freedom outside participation in that which alone is truly free remains an empty word. If Buddhism, in company with every true religion, points the way to freedom, it also tells us the price to be paid for it, failing which there can be only bondage, whether we wish to call that bondage 'freedom' or 'progress' or by any other name.

To complete the present discussion, let us however come back to an aspect of the above question that is relatively external but also, in a certain sense, very actual. There is nothing surprising in the fact that the Japanese reacted in the face of the rationalism of the West and of modern science with its discoveries and inventions in the same way as other peoples who found themselves in similar case; not only in Japan, but in every Eastern country there have been people who doubted their traditional myths and who replaced these, after interpreting them according to the new evolutionary and psychological hypotheses, by other 'myths', false ones this time and lacking in any illuminative or salutary quality. Moreover this prompts the observation that if one were compelled to choose between these allegedly 'scientific' pseudo-myths and an interpretation of the true myths that remains literal, there would be no question but of opting unhesitatingly for the latter, since the literal view, simple as it is, does at least vehicle a virtual knowledge of metaphysical truths – therefore of truths that lie at the very root of our existence and constitute the very essence of our spirit; whereas the would-be 'scientific' interpretation, even if it sometimes contains partial and external truths, lacks what is most essential and furthermore fosters a mentality closed to every kind of superior knowledge. The commonest expression of this mentality is the error of believing that the true myths could have been invented or that a symbol is made to represent a simple phenomenon of nature, therefore merely another symbol; such opinions automatically render a tradition inoperative, in which case it is illogical to pretend to adhere to it seeing one has ceased to understand either its celestial origin or its spiritual language; yet it is tradition that alone gives any sense to life, for man cannot simply draw from out of himself the means that might save him, and even if he does sometimes appear to do so, this is always thanks to tradition and within its framework. Arguments to the contrary, founded upon a supposedly natural morality or on psychological experience, are perfectly illusory.

The Divinities 'are' when human conjectures 'are not'; that is to say, in temporal language, the Divinities 'shall be' in Eternity when all the elaborations of the profane mind shall be no longer.

PART III

VISTAS OF THE MAHĀYĀNA

CHAPTER XIV

TREASURES OF BUDDHISM

WHEN we contemplate a landscape, we absorb its principal features without being distracted by details which, if they were too near, would imprison us, as it were, in their own special nature; in the same way, when we consider one of the great spiritual traditions in order to obtain a general understanding of its fundamental characteristics, none of its essential features escape us and none hides the others from our notice.

Thus, when we come to study the spiritual edifice that is Buddhism, we may discern at its base a message of renunciation and at its summit a message of mystery; in another, more extended dimension we see a message of peace and one of mercy.

The message of renunciation is like a framework for all the rest; it is seen to be the true body of Buddhism, while the element of mystery is its heart; the latter element has found its most direct expression in the Tibetan, Chinese and Japanese forms of the original *Dhyāna* teaching. As for the message of peace, it pervades the whole Buddhist tradition; its central and culminating crystallization is the sacred image of the Buddha, which is found in the Buddhism of the South as well as in that of the North and, within the setting of the latter, in Tibetan as well as in Sino-Japanese Buddhism. The message of mercy, on the other hand, finds general expression through the doctrine of the Bodhisattvas, and a particular and quintessential expression in the doctrine of the Buddha Amitābha (*Amida* in Japanese) where it becomes an invitation to 'the faith that saves'. It supplies a complementary factor of fervour or intensity which rejoins harmoniously the serene detachment that Buddhism propounds in the first place; opposition between these two elements exists in appearance only, for all spiritual realities are united in their common root.

Because modern man lives almost entirely for the things of the senses and from that very fact remains ignorant of the human condition in its totality and in its ultimate purpose it is difficult for him to comprehend the meaning of an attitude seemingly as negative and senseless as that of renunciation; he will merely regard it as a wholly unnatural idea. In reality it can easily be seen that renunciation is not self-explanatory; far from being an end in itself, it only supplies provisional support for the development of an awareness infinitely greater than our *ego*. Renunciation would be purposeless were it not a case of grasping with our whole being, and not with the mind alone, what we really are, and above all of understanding what is total Reality, that 'something' by virtue of which we exist, and from which we cannot for a moment escape. Renunciation aims at preventing man from becoming imprisoned in an ephemeral illusion, from identifying himself with it and finally perishing with it; it aims at helping him to free himself from the tyranny of dreams that leave no outlet. A sage never loses sight of the universal context of life; he does not give himself up to fragments of consciousness such as events agreeable or disagreeable, joyful or sad, for he is perpetually conscious of the whole, so much so that, in the end, the question of renunciation does not even exist for him any longer; he has ceased to be involved in fragmentary experience, he is not bound by it, he does not identify himself with it, nor is he consumed by it.

At this point it might however be objected that man, being alive, cannot avoid psychic or sensual experience; the answer is that in spiritual 'alchemy' there always is, and must be, sufficient allowance made for 'the consolations of the senses', and this in two ways or for two reasons. Firstly, all life, and therefore all effort is subject to rhythm; everything proceeds in waves, by repetition, alternation and compensation, in the soul as in the world; no way can afford to be too negative, for an overstrained bow will snap. Secondly, when a certain degree of awareness of the total Reality or of the 'Void' or 'thusness' (*tathatā*) has been reached, things themselves will allow that Reality to shine through them, despite themselves. The 'consolations of the senses' can conceal Truth and lure us away from it, but they may equally well reveal it and draw us nearer to it, and they cannot help but do so in proportion to the spiritual quality of our perception. This is true, not only of the beauties of nature or of sacred or even simply traditional art, which speak for themselves, but also of bodily satisfactions, in so far as they remain in balance with regard to Heaven and the Dharma.

To the mentality predominating today the idea of peace – of peace interior and transcendent – is no more accessible than that of renunciation. The message of peace refers metaphysically to Pure Being, of which we are as flecks of foam upon its surface; Being is Substance, we are but the accidents. The canonical figure of the Buddha shows us 'that which is' and that which we 'should be', or even that which we 'are' in our eternal reality, for the visible Buddha, just like his own invisible essence, is in conformity with the nature of things. There is activity, since his hands speak to us, but this activity is essentially 'being'; there is an exteriority, since he has a body, but it is nonetheless 'interior'; he is manifest, since he exists but he is 'manifestation of the Void' (*shūnyamurti*). He personifies the Impersonal at the same time as the transcendent or divine Personality of men. When once the veil is torn, the soul returns to its eternal Buddha-nature, just as light, refracted by a crystal, returns to undifferentiated unity when no further obstacle is there to disperse its rays. Pure Existence is in each grain of dust, and it is in this sense that it can be said that a Buddha, or the Buddha, is to be found there.

Peace and beauty dwell at the heart of things. Things, as such, remain 'outside themselves'; if they could dwell completely 'within themselves' they would be identified with the Buddha, in the sense of being immutable and blessed Substance; immutable because free from all opposition, from all causal constraint, from all becoming, and blessed because enjoying the essence of every conceivable beauty and every happiness. The natural symbol of the Buddha is the lotus, a contemplative flower open to the sky and resting on water unruffled by any breath of wind. Peace implies beauty. Beauty is like the sun, it acts without wavering, without intellectual intermediaries, its ways are free, direct, incalculable; like love, with which it is so closely associated, it can heal, unloose, appease, unite or deliver through its simple radiance.

The image of the Buddha is like a drop of the nectar of immortality fallen into the world of forms, or like the sound of that celestial music which could charm a rose tree into flowering amid the snow; such was Sākyamuni, for it is said that the Buddhas bring salvation not only through their teaching but also through their superhuman beauty – and such is his sacramental image.

The image of the Messenger is also that of the Message; there is no essential difference between the Buddha, Buddhism and universal Buddha-nature. Thus, the image points the way, or more exactly its goal, or the human setting for that goal; in other words it displays to us that 'holy sleep' which is all watchfulness and clarity within; by its profound and wondrous 'presence' it suggests 'the stilling of mental agitation and the supreme peace', to quote the words of Shankara.

Two opinions are unacceptable – to pretend as some have done that the life of the Buddha is a 'solar myth' and to pretend that knowledge of the historical Buddha is without importance; this is tantamount, in both cases, to admitting that there can be effects without a cause. Historically, the life of Sākyamuni is too recent, and is much too important, to be dismissed as mere legend; its points of resemblance with more ancient symbolisms serve only to confirm its sacred character. The fact that the Hindus themselves regard the Buddha as an Avatar of Vishnu is additional evidence of his transcendent nature, without which there could be no question of the efficacy of his Law nor of the saving power of his Name. Traditions appear out of the Infinite like flowers; they can no more be invented than can the sacred art which is their witness and their proof.

Peace goes hand in hand with Beauty: the image of the Tathāgata together with his metaphysical and cosmic derivatives and concomitants show that beauty, in its root or essence, is compounded of serenity and compassion; its formal harmony appeals to us because it bespeaks profound goodness and inexhaustible wealth, peace and plenitude.

Like a magnet, the beauty of the Buddha draws all the contradictions of the world and transmutes them into radiant silence. The image that derives from that beauty appears as a drop of the dew of immortality which has fallen into the chilly world of forms and crystallized out in human form, thus being rendered accessible to men.

*

The author's first encounter, intense and unforgettable, with Buddhism and the Far East took place in his childhood when in an ethnographical museum he came upon a great Japanese Buddha of gilded wood, flanked by two images of Kwannon. Finding himself suddenly faced with this vision of majesty and mystery, he might well have paraphrased Caesar by exclaiming *'veni, vidi, victus sum'*. The above reminiscence has been mentioned because of the light it throws on this overwhelming embodiment of an infinite victory of Spirit – on an amazing condensation of the Message in the image of the Messenger – represented by the sacramental statue of the Buddha; Bodhisattva images and other spiritual personifications likewise represent it, such as those Kwannons who seem to have emerged from a celestial river of golden light, silence and mercy.

Every gesture portrayed in images of the Buddhas or Bodhisattvas gives comprehensive expression to the functions of contemplation and teaching; it conveys at the same time light and radiance. Esoteric tradition insists on this character, at once luminous and powerful to save, of the Nirvānic Substance, and conveys this idea through many different symbolisms. The sun is light and heat; similarly, the inner nature of things is truth and mercy. These two qualities are to be found in all that exists, since all that exists is found in them and lives through them; in a sense, they are the Buddha himself, his wisdom, his peace, his compassion and his saving beauty. He is the gateway to the blessed essence of things, and he is the essence itself.

*

Mercy is only the nirvānic beatitude which has fallen and scattered itself over that 'existent nothingness' which is the world. The saving descent of mercy into the soul is a function of our faith, which in turn is a function of our distress, or rather of the degree to which we are aware of it. Our faith, or our trust, thus derives from two sources; the 'lower' one consists of our incapacity to save ourselves from our own wretched state and the other, 'higher' source is the will to save of Amida Buddha, or shall we say of the Buddha in his Amida aspect. On the one hand we must acknowledge our own inability to save ourselves and, on the other, we must be sure that mercy not only 'can' but 'will' save us in function of our faith. Faith streams forth from the depths of our misery and is nourished by the infinite resources of mercy.

Buddhism in its most general and evident aspect, as well as in its most intellectual and esoteric aspect, is founded on 'self-power' (in Japanese *jiriki*); at first sight it appears to leave all initiative to the individual. However, since 'other-power' (*tariki*) is a possibility and indeed a necessity in its own order, Buddhism, as a world message, cannot but include it, be it even by implication only; in fact, the way of 'other-power' occupies a place of its own in the spiritual structure of the Dharma: if Zen and Theravāda are alike in manifesting the first-mentioned aspect of spirituality, the Pure Land doctrine is typical of the latter aspect; but in no case must an irreducible opposition be read into either of these expressions of the Buddhist spirit.

It would be pointless here, and indeed impossible, to admit the hypothesis, upheld by some modern Buddhist writers intent on inter-sectarian polemics, of 'borrowed material',[1] for Truth is One and man is man wherever he may happen to be situated; no profound possibility of man's nature can fail to emerge in some form or other within so vast a framework as that offered by a great Revelation. While Buddhism contains its 'Christian' elements, some apparently 'Buddhist' elements are likewise to be found in Christianity; one can discover some 'Christianity' also in Hinduism, and so forth. Things could not conceivably be otherwise.

All the essential aspects of Truth and of the Way will necessarily be found in a Buddhist climate – with the particularities of emphasis that impose themselves in any given case

[1] There is a well entrenched prejudice, typical of a certain kind of scholarship, which maintains that there can be no coincidences; any text or teaching which resembles another must have been influenced by that other, regardless of probability. This is a mechanical kind of logic and entirely out of keeping with the nature of things. In the present context the allusion is to an opinion which has tried to explain away the redemptive action of Amida, in Pure Land Buddhism, as an interpolation due to Nestorian Christian influences in China at the time when these particular doctrines were beginning to take shape.

– and not one of them can be dispensed with without prejudice to the universality of the Message. We are told in the scriptures that the Buddha makes use of every means to save creatures and that he speaks to each being in a language it can understand, if only it will listen.

The Buddha, once again be it said, is renunciation, peace, mercy and mystery. Mystery is the essence of truth which cannot be adequately conveyed in the language of discursive thought but which may suddenly be made plain in an illuminating flash through a symbol, such as a key-word, a mystic sound, or an image the suggestive action of which may be scarcely understandable. If a holy iconography constitutes one of the most generally effective languages of the spirit, its absence can constitute yet another method. Zen, sparing as it is of the ordinary iconographical appeal, resorts to a highly elliptic and paradoxical *upāya* in the shape of its *koans* – verbal symbols calculated to provoke an ontological breach in our carapace of ignorance, a sudden flash of awareness. In the pictorial art itself a similar attitude can be detected in the mysterious, transparent atmosphere of Taoist and Zen landscapes; the spirit of Zen and that of Tao have met together in this unrivalled art which incidentally combines the ethnic genius of both China and Japan. On this plane of visual contemplation – or contemplative vision – the genius of the Chinese and Japanese is one and the same; no peoples have been more successful in visualizing the mystery to be found at the heart of things. What must, however, not be forgotten in all this is that there will always be one aspect of the whole Truth which allows for the burning up of all forms; the Absolute alone – the ineffable Void – will remain for ever untouched. In this connection Zen contains some highly paradoxical teachings which our present-day iconoclasts, who never understand the symbols they reject, erroneously take quite literally; such truths are not for them.

While the element of mercy has flowered in Jōdo – Shinshu and its Chinese prototype (probably also in the Nichiren school, after a fashion)[1] the element of mystery is perpetuated

---

[1] This school, like the two preceding ones, makes special allowance for the spiritual feebleness of man in our age of latter-day decadence.

in Zen, as we have seen, but it is equally present in Kegon, Tendai and Shingon and their mainland equivalents, not to mention that storehouse of esoteric science to be found in Tibetan Tantricism. Kegon lays stress on the ontological and spiritual homogeneity of the world and on the omnipresence of the Buddha-light, which can be taken as corresponding with the *Buddhi* of Hindu doctrine, at any rate when considered as immanence; Tendai teaches that 'all things can become Buddha', which is one way of saying (to use a Vedāntic term) that all things are *Ātmā* (or Nirvāna) or in other words, that the world, since it is not nothing, is all – it is the Buddha, or Buddha-nature. As for Shingon, it is a metaphysical synthesis as well as a *mantra-yoga* and is thus type-related to Tibetan spiritual ways.

The foregoing considerations must not, however, leave the impression that Theravāda Buddhism is here being under-estimated – indeed far from it; this form of the tradition is all it should be and we must give thanks to heaven that it exists both in its own place and as one among supernatural institutions. Some contemporary apologists for Buddhism try to maintain that its special virtue is its 'natural' or 'human' character; but this betrays a terminological misunderstanding. The 'natural' in Buddhism is supernatural just as the Tathāgata's humanity is superhuman.

*

Many people regard the Buddha, his kind of perfection and his canonical image, as representing an 'a-social' ideal, an eremitic ideal in fact; the hermit is held by many to shirk his 'responsibilities' by pursuing an egotistical goal etc., etc. To begin with, it is absurd to try to define man on the basis of his social value – a human being is neither a bee nor an ant; if fate casts him on a desert island, he will not thereby cease to be a man. Furthermore, social 'responsibilities'[1] (where they are not imaginary) are obviously a relative matter, whereas man's ultimate ends coincide with the Absolute; it is precisely that

[1] Note the hypocritical undertones of the word. In reality the so-called 'useful' man is not sorry to have to remain 'in the world'. If the eremitic way of life be an escape, then so is social moralism; it all depends on what one is escaping from.

ultimate end which is incarnate in the hermit, the contemplative and the Buddha. All human attitudes are 'egotistical', *except* the transcending of the *ego*. The egotism of the species, so marked in the animal world, is no more transcendent than that of the individual, though it counts first biologically and morally. Moreover it must not be forgotten that the *ego*, as a natural factor, has a positive side like any other phenomenon of nature; the injunction 'love thy neighbour as thyself' implies that it is permissible and even necessary – and in any case inevitable – to love one's self. It would be the height of hypocrisy for social theorists to deny the existence of this self-love. Only in Nirvāna is this complex of attitudes, so easily reducible to the absurd, left behind. In Nirvāna there is no self left to love, nor indeed any 'neighbour'; it was with this in mind that Sri Ramana Maharshi was able to say: 'Is the dreamer, when he awakens, supposed to have woken all those of whom he was dreaming?' To transcend the *ego* is to transcend one's human conditioning, though from another point of view such an achievement may be called 'human' in the highest and truest sense inasmuch as it marks man's most typical excellence, his highest aim.

When the reproach of 'egotism' is levelled by those who believe neither in the transcendent Absolute nor in a hereafter, the argument becomes like a dialogue between two deaf people; but when that same reproach comes from professing 'believers' it is worth reminding them that the 'good' which the individual can do to society, like society itself and the individual as such, operates on a cosmic plane that gives rise to 'evil' and cannot fail to do so. Suffering is not by its own nature opposed to salvation any more than pleasure or wealth are opposed to perdition, if one may allow oneself a truism which religious 'believers' themselves are unfortunately choosing more and more to disregard. Suffering is not merely a kind of bad luck which we can hope to eliminate through 'progress' after thousands of years of mysterious impotence. One can transcend Samsāra, but one cannot abolish it. It is more worthy to save souls than to save bodies, though the latter activity is not to be despised and indeed can be included in the former, but only on condition that the superior claims of the former task are always clearly borne in mind.

Now to save others one must first be able to save one's self, if we may so put it; there is no other way of communicating the 'absolute good', in the sight of which the distinction between 'self' and 'not-self' can moreover hardly be said to have any meaning. Finally, one cannot save a soul as one would pull somebody out of the water; one can only rescue those who are willing to be rescued, and that is why it is ridiculous to reproach the religions for not having succeeded in saving a world that persistently disregards their teachings and their warnings.

Contemplative solitude is most visibly incarnate in the person of the hermit, hence the frequent accusation that he is 'useless' or 'unproductive' – to use a still more despicable and barbarous term; in reality, nothing is more useful than to demonstrate in concrete form the value of the Absolute and the grievous vanity of transient things. The hermit exercises the greatest possible charity since, the question of his own deliverance apart, he points the way towards that which has the highest value, and in a final analysis, the only value. It may be objected, what would then become of society if everyone decided to be a hermit? The answer is, firstly, that the question of what would become of society is of secondary importance, since society does not bear within itself its own justifying cause – it represents no unconditional values; and secondly, if everyone were to follow the hermit's example, or were ready to do so, the world would be saved in any case, subsidiary considerations being then governed by essentials. Thirdly, to treat the question in more specific terms, we should remember that there have always been saints engaged in the affairs of the world, men such as Shōtoku Taishi, the holy Prince Regent who introduced Buddhism into Japan and saw that it took firm root there, and king Song-tsen Gampo who rendered the same service to the Tibetans early in the seventh century A.D., also Hōjō Tokimune the governor who resisted the Mongol invasion of the Japanese islands – one of the greatest figures in their history and in Zen; nor must we forget the Emperor Asoka who provides the very pattern of the dedicated ruler, Dharma Raja:[1] none of these secular leaders found any cause to blame the hermits – far from it – and indeed

---

[1] Similarly, in Christendom, we have Charlemagne, St Louis, Joan of Arc' St Alexander Nevsky, to name only a few.

could never have done so, in view of the high example of so many solitary contemplatives. The hermit's message is not about rocks and trees, it concerns detachment from the impermanent and attachment to the Eternal; the hermit exemplifies, not a contingency but a principle; he demonstrates the superiority of contemplation over action (even when the latter surrounds the former, as in the teaching of the Bhagavadgita) and of 'being' over 'doing', of truth over works.

Man belongs above all to the Absolute – the same holds good whether we speak of the Void (*Shūnya*), Extinction (*Nirvāna*) or God – and face to face with the Absolute he is always alone. From another point of view, it can be said that in the presence of the Infinite there is no solitude.

Nirvāna is Truth in its pure state; in it all relative and partial truths are absorbed. Errors must continue to exist so long as their merely relative potential, their *karma*, has not been exhausted, but as regards the Absolute they have never been and never will be. On their own level they are what they are, but the last word shall remain with the silence of the eternal Ādi-Buddha.

CHAPTER XV

MYSTERY OF THE BODHISATTVA

THERE is a side of Buddhism which makes it akin to the Semitic religions – paradoxically so, considering its non-theistic character – in the sense that its starting point is related to a human point of view rather than to the metaphysical nature of things. When, for instance, it is said that Existence is but suffering and that the Absolute is the cessation of suffering, and further that human perfection lies in 'compassion for all living beings', this does indeed open up a perspective conformable to our human situation and to our ultimate interests, but it does not straightway give the most direct possible definition of 'that which is', if one can thus describe a thought which seeks to embrace at the same time both the manifested Universe and that which surpasses it.

Such an observation is not, however, of a kind that logically need embarrass Buddhists,[1] and this for two reasons; firstly, because they are in no danger of overlooking the fact that the doctrines of the Buddhas are only 'celestial mirages' intended to catch, as in a golden net, the greatest possible number of creatures plunged in ignorance, suffering and transmigration, and that it is therefore the benefit of creatures and not the suchness of the Universe which determines the contingent form which the Buddhist Message must take; and secondly, because Buddhism, within the framework of its own wisdom, reaches beyond 'the letter' of a formal 'mythology' and ultimately transcends all possible human powers of expression, thus realizing a degree of contemplative disinterestedness not surpassed by the Vedānta, Taoism or any other purely metaphysical doctrine.

[1] Neither need the anthropomorphism of their own Scriptures embarrass Christians, if they will but read with intelligence.

Hence the question that Sākyamuni might have asked himself – if he had had to ask one – was, 'Which is the most effective way of conveying the saving Truth to men in these latter times?' and not 'Which is the most adequate (or least inadequate) formulation of the metaphysical nature of things?'

Neither the Vedānta nor Neo-Platonism include the possibility of addressing their teaching effectively to all men and thus of serving as the vehicle of an entire tradition, nor indeed is this their purpose. But Buddhism of necessity has to envisage this possibility, and it cannot therefore fail to offer itself first of all as an *upāya*, a 'provisional means', for pursuing an objective which is above all charitable, in the widest and most complete sense of that word. Buddhists, it must be stressed, are all the better equipped for the recognition of this need since they are very far from claiming that the truth of Nirvāna can be enclosed in a definitive sense within the mould of any dialectic whatsoever. Nevertheless there results from this general situation, and apart from any fluctuations of terminology, a certain difficulty in speaking of Knowledge in such a way as to satisfy at one and the same time the demands of metaphysical truth and of that side of Buddhism which is concerned with the human will and human emotions.

*

Primitive Buddhism distinguishes extrinsically between a *Samyaksam-Buddha* and a *Pratyeka-Buddha;* the former corresponds to what Hindus would call a major Avatāra, having by definition the function of 'founder of a religion', and the latter to a *Jīvan-Mukta* – a man 'delivered in his lifetime' – who neither has the quality of a major or plenary Avatāra nor consequently the function attaching to such a one; and not having had a Buddha as master, neither does he have disciples. After this comes the *Srāvaka* or 'hearer' who is a disciple, or the disciple of a disciple of the Buddha; like the Pratyeka-Buddha, he is an Arahant or perfected saint, but is such thanks to the direct influence of the Master, if one may so put it. Finally there is the *Bodhisattva* who, in principle, is a saint destined for Buddhahood.

Now, when it is stated, as in the Mahāyāna writings, that

the condition of a Pratyeka-Buddha is inferior to that of a Bodhisattva because the realization of the former is 'self-centred' and lacks compassion for creatures, it seems to be forgotten – or at least this logical objection obtrudes itself *a priori* – that Nirvāna implies by definition the abolition of all egoity and the realization of total charity. This is an objection which the Mahāyāna itself raises in its own way and in its sapiential dimension; but this does not imply any contradiction if it be remembered that two truths here are recognized, the one being relative and provisional and the other absolute and final and that the doctrinal form of the Mahāyāna is essentially apophatic and antinomic. In other words, when it is said that the Mahāyāna is 'great' (*mahā*) for the sole reason that its aim is the salvation of 'all living beings' thanks to the sacrificial ideal of the Bodhisattva – and not the salvation of a single individual as is the case with the Hīnayāna or 'lesser vehicle' – then it is proper to object, in accordance with the higher teaching of the Mahāyāna itself, that the alleged reason carries no weight with respect to Nirvāna or, what amounts to the same thing, with respect to Knowledge; not to mention the fact that this world of ignorance and suffering, Samsāra, the Round of Existence, is metaphysically necessary and has not to be considered solely from a volitional and emotional angle.

However that may be, the Mahāyāna under its sapiential aspect aims at maintaining its solidarity with the heroic ideal of the Bodhisattva, while nonetheless referring back that ideal to a strictly metaphysical perspective. It first declares that Compassion is a dimension of Knowledge, then it adds that one's 'neighbour' is non-real and that charity must therefore be exercised 'quietly when the occasion arises' and without slipping into the dualist and objectivist illusion, for, as it says, there is no one whom our charity could concern, nor is there a charity which could be 'ours'. In this way, though taking the compassionate interpretation of the Bodhisattva's function for its starting point, the gnosis of the Mahāyāna follows a roundabout route to rejoin the most rigorous, and therefore the most objective and disinterested metaphysical positions.

To speak as precisely as possible, Buddhism can be said to

present itself under the following fundamental aspects: first of all, primitive Buddhism; then Theravāda Buddhism which is its continuation as to form if not as to content; finally, Mahāyāna (the 'Great Vehicle') which qualifies whatever preceded it as Hīnayāna ('Lesser Vehicle') and which in its general form exalts the heroic ideal of the Bodhisattva; then, within the actual framework of the Mahāyāna, a sapiential perspective which corrects and counterbalances the elements of 'love' as specifically embodied in the mahāyānic ideal; while parallel with this perspective there is another which is devotional and centred particularly on the cult of the Buddha Amitābha as found in China and Japan. If then the 'greatness' of the Great Vehicle be admitted, this is not for the sake of the altruistic ideal which appears as its mythological mantle and its elementary thesis, but because of the two quintessences just mentioned – the one sapiential and the other devotional – the ultimate crystallizations of which are, in Japan, Zen and Jōdo.

While maintaining solidarity with the sacrificial ideal of its basic thesis, but without following it into its literal and too human interpretations, the sapiential Mahāyāna adopts the terminology of this thesis and projects into it its own certainties. Consequently it will say, not that Nirvāna requires charity to complete it but that the condition of the Pratyeka-Buddha is not Nirvāna in the fullest sense, or that it is a Nirvāna on a transitory level; in which case, the use here of the title 'Buddha' seems to indicate a change of terminology, since it is *a priori* abnormal to call a man Buddha when he is placed lower than a Bodhisattva. It is however possible to justify such a use of this title seeing that it refers to a state which is already nirvānic in the sense that there is 'extinction' at least in relation to the formal world, this by itself being enough to dispense the one concerned from any further obligation to return to the round of births and deaths.

The mahāyānist polemic against the Pratyeka-Buddhas should therefore not astonish us unduly, springing as it does from a perspective of sacrificial idealism. To mention a parallel case in Hindusim, the Vishnuite *bhakti*, which is also a way of Love, often represents the Shivaite *jnāni* (gnostic) as being a rationalist, sterile, sad and lacking what is essential until one day, touched by Grace, he discovers devotional love – as if the latter were not already, and eminently, comprised in Gnosis itself.

In considering the Bodhisattvic ideal, account must be taken of the following fundamental situation: Buddhism unfolds itself in a sense between the empirical notions of suffering and cessation of suffering; the notion of Compassion springs from this very fact and is an inevitable or necessary link in what might be called the spiritual mythology of the Buddhist tradition. The fact of suffering and the possibility of putting an end to it must needs imply compassion, unless a man were living alone upon the earth. This is where the Bodhisattva enters on the scene: he incarnates the element of compassion – the ontological link as it were between Pain and Felicity – just as the Buddha incarnates Felicity and just as ordinary beings incarnate suffering; he must be present in the cosmos as long as there is both a Samsāra and a Nirvāna, this presence of his being expressed by the statement that the Bodhisattva wishes to deliver 'all beings'.

From a more contingent point of view, it could also be admitted that concern for personal salvation, while irreproachable in itself, does in practice involve a certain danger of egotism when acknowledged by a numerous collectivity in which exoteric tendencies are bound to manifest themselves; from this angle the intervention of the Mahāyāna ideal is seen to be providential. At the time when it first appeared on the scene in specific form the Buddhist tradition had doubtless begun to be affected by all kinds of narrow and pharisaical currents; the same had applied to Brahmanism in the Buddha's time as also to Judaism at the time of Christ; which does not mean, however, that either of these traditions had succumbed entirely or in regard to their innermost life. For this reason also there can be no question nowadays of applying the polemic of the ancient Mahāyānists to the Theravādins of Ceylon, Burma and Indo-China.

Furthermore, concerning the tradition itself when regarded in a more fundamental sense, the very necessity of its developing an emotional element, in the absence of a theism properly so called

and given the conditons of the 'latter times',[1] explains the oppor-
tuneness of the cult of the Bodhisattva in correlation with the
way of works and the way of love; in this respect, the difference
between the Buddhism of the North and that of the South is no
more than one of style and 'mythology'; it in no wise affects
their common supra-formal essence. To give one particular
illustration, it can be admitted that, if, for instance, in the
climate of the Mahāyāna the Buddha Amitābha has become
the object of a quasi-personal cult, this is because, as
Bodhisattva, he has been able to accumulate the merits capable
of creating a 'Buddha-field' and a 'Pure Land'; but this retro-
spective motive evidently need not affect contemplation,
whether in its devotional or its gnostic dimension, and especially
since the same causal connection may also be conceived as
working in the opposite direction: this is the same as saying
that here the 'prime mover' is not a contingency like the merit
accumulated by an individual (or by a 'karmic nexus' if one so
prefers), but a principle of Mercy that creates at the same time
both the merit itself and the saint who accumulates the merit.
The principle of Mercy results from the very nature of the
Ādi-Buddha, the Absolute who is at the same time both
Knowledge and Love.

To return to our previous illustration, the doctrine of
Shinran provides a wonderful synthesis between the ways of
devotion and wisdom: to start with, he envisages the 'Pure
Land', the Paradise Sukhāvati, in its aspect of transcendence,
hence of identity with Nirvāna; similarly, he reminds us that,
by virtue of universal analogies, death can serve to rend the
veil of *Māyā* or existential illusion, and hence can also be an
occasion for Illumination and Deliverance; but this depends on
one's being in a spiritual state which allows this junction to be
effected or this analogy to be actualized, and this precisely is

[1] According to the *Nirvāna-Sūtra*, 'those who despise the Dharma will then
be like the volume of the earth of the ten directions, and those who remain
faithful to it will be like the crumb of earth that can be put on a finger-nail'.
And similarly according to the *Saddharma-Pundarika* 'At the horrible time of
the end, men will be malevolent, false, evil and obtuse and they will imagine
they have reached perfection when it will be nothing of the sort'. Under such
circumstances a spiritual treasure can no longer be imposed collectively except
by means of a sentimental, even a passion-rousing, element, which alone is
capable of acting effectively in a medium of this kind.

made possible by the Grace of Amitābha and by our confidence in it; the whole stress here is laid on the element of 'faith' (which is not without analogy, *mutatis mutandis*, with the *satori* of Zen[1]) and this faith is a confidence which, by its quality, coincides with perfect disregard of the *ego*. The Absolute – which here has revealed itself under the particular name of Amitābha – is essentially Wisdom and Compassion, Knowledge and Mercy; that is to say, in the symbolism of the Buddha Amitābha the 'original vow' not to enter Nirvāna except on condition that those who invoke the sacred Name with faith should be saved is in fact the Absolute's aspect of Mercy; it is as if the Absolute were paraphrasing the vow and saying: 'I would not wish to possess Beatitude if there existed between Me and contingent beings an insurmountable barrier preventing them from drinking of my Beatitude'; or again: 'I would not be the Absolute were I not blissful and merciful'.

But this way of Amitābha of which Shinran, following his predecessor Hōnen, was the great spokesman, likewise includes, short of the nirvānic miracle of which we have spoken, a properly human finality: it opens out on the Paradise Sukhāvati where the faithful will await Nirvāna till the end of the cycle. This Paradise is of a quite different order from the happy realms comprised in the Round of Transmigration; it is exactly equivalent to the Paradise of the Semitic religions, in which 'eternity' means precisely this nirvānic conclusion and the ceasing of samsāric rebirth.

*

A distinction must be made between the personal trans-migratory Bodhisattva and the celestial or universal Bodhisattva endowed with ubiquity; the former, if he be not simply a manifestation of the latter, accumulates merits by his virtues and his actions; the latter is the cosmic emanation of a Buddha, or, in western terms, he is the Archangel who

[1] It has been possible to say in Zen: 'If you meet the Buddha, slay him'. This means (paraphrasing the first phrase in the *Tao-Te-King* – 'the Tao that can be grasped is not the real Tao'): the Buddha whom you can meet is not the real Buddha. This gives the point of view of the absolute Subject, infinitely transpersonal therefore; perfect non-objectivation is the keynote of this way of seeing things.

manifests a given Divine Quality; his reintegration into Nirvāna coincides with the *Mahāpralaya*, the Apocatastasis which effects the return of all manifestation to the Principle or of all contingency to the Absolute. The human Bodhisattva can be (to use Hindu terminology) either a *bhakta* or a *jnāni*: in the former case the way is shared between devotion and compassion – devotion in respect of the Buddhas and celestial Bodhisattvas and compassion towards the creatures wandering in Samsāra – whilst in the latter case it is the way of gnosis that takes precedence over everything else. Here compassion is not something added in sentimental fashion to a supposedly imperfect mode of knowledge; on the contrary compassion is regarded as the secondary dimension or internal complement of a knowledge which is virtually or effectively perfect, because it is situated on the axis of Buddhahood or is identified with Buddhahood itself.[1]

Some will doubtless object that the gnosis of the Bodhisattva is not that of the Buddha: whereas the compassion of the latter is intrinsic in the sense that he carries all things in himself, the universal pity of the Bodhisattva is extrinsic and therefore still situated under the sign of duality. This view, however, does not do full justice to the nature of the great Bodhisattvas, whose sacrificial sojourn in the world is an occasion for realizing Nirvāna in a certain sense within the samsāric condition itself. This must needs be so, for the simple reason that a being cannot deprive himself, from life to life, of that very Enlightenment which constitutes the meaning and the end of all his efforts, all his virtues and all his merits. It is neither possible on the one

[1] A Buddhist friend has rightly pointed out to the author that the merits, compassion and knowledge of the Bodhisattva correspond respectively to *karma*, *bhakti* and *jnāna* and consequently are addressed to those who follow those ways; for each of them the Bodhisattva reveals himself under a particular aspect. To use Buddhist terms, these are the three aspects called *upekshā* ('passionlessness'), *maitrī* ('love of one's neighbour') and *prajnā* ('knowledge'). In the framework of gnosis, compassion nevertheless changes its mode: Jacques Bacot was justified when, in his introduction to '*Le Poète tibétain Milarepa*', he declared that 'Buddhic pity has no relationship with sensibility. It is entirely objective, cool and connected with a metaphysical conception. It is not spontaneous, but the outcome of long meditations. The idealism which tends no longer to differentiate between "me" and "not-me" is the generator of this pity for all that lives and is the victim of illusion'. It is the compassion necessarily comprised in *prajnā* itself.

hand to persist in an exclusively negative situation nor, on the other, to regard the ultimate Wisdom merely as a means of coming to another's aid, which would amount in effect to making a means of the end or a contingency of the Absolute; Knowledge as such cannot be an instrument designed for charity any more than the Real can be subordinate to the illusory: as the Tibetan Arahant Milarepa put it 'one should not show oneself rash and hasty in the intention to serve others as long as one has not realized the Truth oneself; otherwise one risks becoming a blind man leading the blind'. The condition of the gnostic Bodhisattva would be neither conceivable nor tolerable if it were not a matter of contemplating the Absolute in the heart and in the world at one and the same time. Above all it must be stressed that Knowledge, by definition, has no connection with the quantity of merits or the number of incarnations. This is what Zen teaches in the most uncompromising manner: texts like the *Diamond Sūtra* or the Chinese *Sutra of Huang-Po* formulate the decisive truth in the most explicit possible fashion and thereby express, in terms of doctrine, the very quintessence of Buddhism. Only a bhaktism with an exoteric bias could imagine perfect Knowledge as being the fruit of a process of accumulating elements of one kind or another; one must not let oneself be deceived on that score even if these elements appear sublime from the human point of view; in short there is nothing quantitative or moral about the Spirit. According to the *Lankavatāra-sūtra*, the Bodhisattvas, while holding back from entry into Nirvāna, are there already in fact, 'for in their love and compassion there is no cause of illusory distinction and consequently no intervention of such distinction'. The *Diamond Sūtra* mentions this saying of the Buddha: 'A Bodhisattva who says: "I will deliver all beings" must not be called a Bodhisattva'.

Something should be said about the distinction between Nirvāna and Parinirvāna: only death allows of a total reintegration (for those who in their lifetime have realized 'Extinction') in that 'Supreme Extinction' which is none other than the Vedantine Selfhood. Living beings, whatever may be their degree of spirituality, remain of necessity linked with Being, which belongs to the realm of Nirvāna since it represents a perfect transcendence in relation to all manifestation and to the whole cosmic enmeshment, but which, being still of the realm of *Māyā* whereof it is the summit or quintessence, is not yet the Self. If in a certain respect death brings no change for one who has realized Nirvāna it nonetheless in another respect effects a considerable change, so that it can be said that death for the 'living liberated one' is neither a modification nor a non-modification, or that it is both at once. However, if we say that the Buddha, in dying, entered Parinirvāna, this is again only an earthly mode of speech: in reality, he was always there in his capacity of *Dharmakāya*, 'body of the Dharma'; similarly he did not cease to dwell in Heaven in his capacity of *Sambhogakāya*, 'body of Bliss', even while he was manifest among mortals by virtue of *Nirmanakāya*, the 'body of super-natural metamorphosis'. In monotheistic terms it can be said that to every Prophet there corresponds an Archangel and, beyond creation, a divine Name, and that every divine Name reflects in its own way the Divinity one and undivided.

An important point touching the mystery of the Bodhisattva in his capacity of a 'virtual Buddha' is the comprehension of the nirvānic essence of Samsāra: just as it has been said elsewhere that the finite is a sort of internal dimension of the Infinite – an indispensably necessary dimension, by reason of the intrinsic character of infinity – with equal justice Samsāra could here be defined as a sort of dimension of Nirvāna, or an 'ignorant' manner (in the sense of the Indian term *avidyā*, nescience) of envisaging the latter, the factor of 'ignorance' being called forth by the very infinity of the divine 'Voidness'. The actual substance of this 'reality in reverse' is constituted by those countless 'grains of sand' which are the *dharmas*, the elementary qualities, these being like the segmented, innumer-able and inverted crystallizations of the Void or of the pure nirvānic Substance. The 'impermanence' of things is none other than their own relativity.

*

To sum up what has just been explained and at the same time to complete it, it is necessary to distinguish between three Nirvānas or three degrees of Extinction, two of which are still in the order of *Māyā* or of contingency while the third, Parinirvāna, coincides with the Absolute; if the word Nirvāna referred to the Absolute regardless of context Parinirvāna would spell a redundancy devoid of meaning. The primary Nirvāna is ontologically that of the Bodhisattva: it is extinction in relation to formal manifestation and corresponds to the degree of Archangels, Heaven, Existence; the word 'ontologically' applies here because the Bodhisattva still lives at this level even if he has already realized the second Nirvāna spiritually, the one which coincides with the state of the terrestrial *Buddha*, that is to say with extinction in regard to universal manifestation; positively expressed the latter realization corresponds to the degree of pure Being. The third Nirvāna, beyond *Māyā*, is that of the celestial or absolute Buddha: this is Parinirvāna, extinction in relation to Being or to *Māyā* and corresponds to the supreme Self of the Vedantines. Now when it is said that the Bodhisattva renounces Nirvāna this means that he intends to remain, not in formal manifestation alone, but in transmigration, whatever be the degree of extinction that he may inwardly have attained. What the Bodhisattva aims at is a perfection not 'divine' but 'cosmic', one which will result in his obtaining a 'divine mission' or 'message'; now this function – that of Samyaksam-Buddha – requires a perfection of *cosmic* Knowledge which the Pratyeka-Buddha does not possess and which moreover is, like the fact of Revelation itself, devoid of importance in regard to absolute Knowledge. The Bodhisattva can only 'renounce' Nirvāna on condition of having attained it in the mode accessible within formal existence, and it is only then that his aspiration to become a Samyaksam-Buddha has an intrinsic meaning; prior to that, his desire even to 'become a Buddha' or to 'save all living beings' is ambivalent, being at the same time a stimulus and an obstacle, depending on whether his way is primarily conditioned by Love or Knowledge, *bhakti* or *jnāna*. On attaining Nirvāna he will know whether the Ādi-Buddha, the supreme Buddha personifying the nirvānic Infinite, has chosen him or not, or in other words whether the universal economy, or the equilibrium and rhythm of the Cosmos, has decided that he is to be a Messenger or else that he is to be integrated, pending the completion of a Cosmic

Cycle or *kalpa*, in the state and function of an Archangel, such as Avalokiteshvara or Manjusrī.

The Enlightenment which occurred in the lifetime of Sakyamuni beneath the Bodhi tree is none other than what in Western parlance would be called 'Revelation', that is to say the reception of the Message or the assuming of the prophetic function: this Revelation is summed up in the very elliptic formula of the Bodhi of Sakyamuni: 'That being, which becomes, from the becoming of this, which becomes; that non-becoming, which does not become, from the cessation of this which ceases'. To which may be added the well-known commentary: 'Of those things which proceed from a cause the Tathāgata has explained the cause and likewise their cessation the great Pilgrim has declared'. Just as the soul descends suddenly on the embryo once it is sufficiently formed – neither before nor after – so Enlightenment descends on the Bodhisattva who has acquired, side by side with his Knowledge and his Nirvāna, those specific cosmic perfections which the shining forth of a Revealer requires.

At the risk of repetition it is necessary to return here to a particularly important point: if there is in the Mahāyāna an element which calls for some caution from the metaphysical point of view it is not, of course, the vocation of the Bodhisattva as such but, what is quite different, the Bodhisattvic ideal in so far as this is polemically opposed to the 'non-altruistic' spirituality of the pure contemplative, as if, firstly, all true spirituality did not necessarily include charity, and secondly, as if the consideration of some contingency or other could enter into competition with pure and total Knowledge. Moreover, if the wish to deliver all beings, as expressed under this elementary and even sentimental form, is of necessity opposed to Knowledge – one might describe it as 'interested disinterestedness[1] – one may well ask what, from the point of view of tradition, can be the profound meaning or the alchemical function of a desire objectively so disproportionate and subjectively so contingent? The answer is that here is a means of 'canalising' certain mentalities towards virtue and truth: it is this heroic abnega-

[1] Conversely, the actionless solitude of the contemplative could be described as 'disinterested interest'.

tion, this heroism expressed at one and the same time as beneficent action and love which is calculated, like nothing else, to attract men of goodwill and to enflame them, and this is a factor that tradition must needs take into account in its many-sided formulation. As for the Bodhisattva himself, his refusal of Nirvāna – not of the 'nirvānic axis' which passes through him, but of the ultimate repose in Extinction – is simply the will to be reborn despite the ability not to be reborn; since the former possibility exists and is offered to him, he has a right to accept it consonantly with his own vocation and destiny. What then the Bodhisattva lacks is not the formless, nor even the supra-existential Nirvāna – that which the terrestrial Buddha enjoys – but only the 'mandate of prophecy' which would make him into a Samyaksam-Buddha, while at the same time entailing his final retirement into unmanifest, and hence extra-samsāric Reality. The absence of such a 'mandate' is evidently involuntary, whereas staying in transmigration is vocational and aims either expressly at obtaining the 'mandate' or 'mission', or else at a state of beneficent and 'angelic' presence in the Samsāra. It is this and this alone which is meant by the refusal to enter into Nirvāna, since it is obvious that no one can prevent, or could wish to prevent, the flowering forth of Knowledge.

Humanly speaking, the Bodhisattva is an altogether extraordinary being owing to the acuteness, amplitude and scope of his faculties, something which on this scale cannot be the case with the Pratyeka-Buddha, who, although 'delivered in this life' and possessing supreme Knowledge to the extent that it can be imparted to one still bound to the earthly or formal condition, may only be endowed with individual faculties which – apart from intellectuality and contemplativity – do not really go beyond the general norm, as the example of a Rāmakrishna or of a Rāmana Maharshi goes to show; leaving aside their inner realization, their human breadth – which is the sole consideration here – is obviously less than that of a Rāma or a Krishna, or of the young prince Siddhârtha, the future Buddha; here there is no common measure, and even the mightiest genius is nothing in comparison with this order of greatness, speaking uniquely from the point of view of human constitution and without bringing in any later spiritual consequences. Or take the example of the Mother of Jesus: tradition tells us that in a natural – or 'supernaturally natural' – manner she possessed every virtue and all science in the fullest possible measure; this supereminent perfection was indispensable for her role as 'coredemptress', but it is a case of providential ordering or cosmic bountifulness which, while necesssarily joined at a certain point to Knowledge, is nonetheless not the prerequisite for it, otherwise it would be pointless to speak of gnosis and to teach it to mere mortals. The 'superhumanly human' perfection of the Bodhisattva is necessary, not for Knowledge as such and thus for going beyond this world, but for the earthly manifestation of the Divine Principle, of the liberating Truth, of Nirvāna – which is an altogether different matter; far from being exclusively directed towards the unmanifest, the human nature – actually, angelic – of the virtual Buddha on the contrary unfolds in the cosmos, as the sun illumines the night. It must be stressed that this is what renders his nature capable of conveying that crystallization of the Infinite – or that Truth 'become flesh' – which is Revelation, the seed and nourishment of a universal and millenary tradition.

As to whether this perfection, combined with the *Bodhi* for which it is the predisposed receptacle, constitutes a degree of Knowledge, the answer is both yes and no; it is as if one were to ask whether the Samsāra is real; the answer can be either affirmative or negative, depending on the viewpoint, provided that the absolute truth be acknowledged. 'Everything is *Atmā*,' to be sure, but 'the world is false, *Brahma* is true', and 'there is no divinity except the one Divinity'. The problem basically comes down to the 'divine character' of *Māyā*, or the nature of *Māyā* as 'modality', 'play', 'unveiling' or 'aspect' of the ineffable Self, of *Paramātmā*. The 'supreme Knowledge' attributed to the *Samyaksam-Buddha* comprises essentially three factors: the unimaginable cosmic deployment of the perfection of the Bodhisattva, secondly Nirvāna as comprised in that perfection, and finally the 'celestial burden' of Revelation, Dharma; as for knowing whether extra-nirvānic factors, however incomparable they may seem at their respective levels, add something to Nirvāna or themselves constitute an element of principial Knowledge, this seems to be a question which metaphysically answers itself.

There is nonetheless a factor which allows one to accept, with the necessary reservations, the current interpretations of the Illumination of the Samyaksam-Buddha as a degree – or as the supreme degree – of Knowledge, and it is the following: in the Bodhisattva who is ready to receive it, Revelation coincides with the 'recollection' of a Wisdom 'previously' acquired, but transitorily 'forgotten' through the very fact of incarnation. This forgetfulness or this initial disorder occurs for the simple reason that it is not in this new world of forms that the Bodhisattva had acquired his Wisdom; the passing obscuration in question is moreover comparable, in the natural order, to infancy which also transitorily veils faculties which are nonetheless pre-existing. Under the Bodhi tree there was therefore a double Illumination; on the one hand the 'recollection' which was bound to occur by force of circumstances after the inevitable gropings of a new body in a new space, and on the other hand the Revelation accompanied by that cosmic Knowledge which characterizes the Samyaksam-Buddha. If we admit that the term 'Buddha' can have two or more senses, as the Mahāyāna obliges us to do, we must equally admit two or more kinds of Bodhi; there is one Bodhi which belongs to every Buddha, be he externally Bodhisattva or not, and there is another *Bodhi* which concerns solely the Buddha as Revealer and in which an extrinsic dimension is blended with his intrinsic Enlightenment.

The Bodhisattva who has become Buddha possesses absolute knowledge not by virtue of his quality of Samyaksam-Buddha, but by virtue of his quality of Arahant or fully perfected saint; that is to say he can be, but does not have to be Samyaksam-Buddha because he enjoys this Knowledge. It is also evident that the illusory opposition between Samsāra and Nirvāna exists only from the point of view of the world and is resolved only in and by Nirvāna and not otherwise, for in this matter there is no possibility of any reciprocity or symmetry, so that the particular science of the Buddha in his capacity of

Revealer could add nothing whatever to nirvānic Knowledge as such.

Tradition records that the Buddha wished at first to keep the Revelation (or the corresponding Knowledge) to himself, and it was only after the thrice repeated insistence of the gods that he decided to communicate it; this initial hesitation is deeply symbolic, for it manifests an aspect of the very process of revelation, rather like the breaking of the first Tablets of the Law by Moses on Sinai. Later, he declared that he had hidden nothing, but had on the contrary made the Truth radiant as the daylight which illumines everything. This saying, far from contradicting the graded plurality of meanings in the sacred teaching, as some imagine, really affirms the universality and totality of the Dharma; even the most subtle aspects of the Truth have been expressed with a clarity sufficient for 'those who have ears to hear'; the teaching has yielded all the keys necessary, if only in the form of a flower in the hand of the Tathāgata, that flower which was the origin of Zen. Moreover of no truth can it be said that it is esoteric in itself; it can only be so described in relation to a particular degree of understanding. Now the source of incomprehension resides more often in the will than in the intelligence; that is to say the obstacles are above all to be found in the realm of the passions taken in the broadest sense, which brings us back in fact to the distinction between the two kinds of limitation, the one fundamental and the other accidental, and to the problem of their mutual tangling in human nature, or again, in other words, to the question of knowing to what extent an apparent substance is accidental or whether an appearance of accident denotes on the contrary a substance.

When we say that the Buddha's Revelation is accompanied by a concrete and penetrating consciousness of the rhythms of Samsāra – of the world as an indefinite chain of causes and effects – it must be clearly understood that the kind or *style* of this knowledge depends on the style of the Revelation which it accompanies: whatever the Revelation declares becomes immediately known to the Avatāra without its being always possible to assign a priority, in the avatāric soul, either to the

Knowledge itself or to the 'divine fact' of the Revelation. As for the question of spiritual style, it is for example possible to know space in diverse ways and starting from different symbolisms by applying different measures: it can be known in terms of a circle, a cross, a star or a spiral and it is thus that Samsāra can be known according to diverse perspectives, analogically speaking; but this Knowledge will always have a character which is no more than a 'relative absoluteness', like every reflection of the absolute in the contingent.

Monotheism seems to teach that the world has a beginning and not an end while Buddhism, for its part, seems to assert that the world has an end, but had no beginning. The above remark made by a Buddhist to the writer calls for the following comment: the answer to both difficulties is contained in the idea of Apocatastasis, which satisfies the demands of both the above metaphysics by bringing creation to an end – but without annihilation, quite the contrary – and by realizing the humanly impossible ideal of the Bodhisattvas. When Buddhists admit that Samsāra will come to an end thanks to the Bodhisattvas and Buddhas who will have saved 'all living beings' down to the last blade of grass, they implicitly attribute the final reintegration to the Ādi-Buddha, the universal or divine Buddha whose *act* is in effect identified with the transmutative Logos. In other words, the Apocatastasis or *Mahāpralaya* is the Bodhi – the passage to the state of Buddha – of all celestial Bodhisattvas, such as Avalokitēshvara, Manjusri, Kshitigarbha, Akashagarbha; the nirvānic light which submerges, penetrates, transmutes and devours Samsāra is their illumination saving the Universe; and in fact it is through the celestial Essences that this Light will act, before re-absorbing them in their turn in its infinite Silence.

In Buddhism, which is refractory to speculations of a literalist kind, language seeks to communicate or release a state of 'being' rather than a 'thought': understanding and being tend to be merged as far as this is possible, whence the wide use of *upāyas*, 'instrumental concepts', of which the justification is not so much a truth conceived in the abstract as an inward transformation and intuition which is in a sense 'existential', if such a paradox be permissible. Thus the idea of the

Bodhisattva has for its aim to destroy egotism, and then the ego itself; perhaps fundamentally the Mahāyāna reproaches its conventionally conceived Hīnayānist opponents less with an imperfection of doctrine than with one of method; that is to say it considers that the ideal of Bodhi is in practice unrealizable without the concurrent ideal of the Bodhisattva which alone is capable of cutting the Gordian knot of egoity. Other views can assuredly be held on this point; but however that may be, if the Bodhisattva is supposed to save all sentient beings, this indicates above all a total gift of self, hence a perfect victory over the *ego*. Compassion then appears as the criterion of authenticity in respect of Knowledge; the same applies to love in Christian gnosis, for which wisdom without love is but 'sounding brass, or a tinkling cymbal'. Thus regarded, 'love' is that which enables 'understanding' to pass into 'being', or that which attaches us ontologically to Truth and thus opens us to the transforming magic of the Symbol.

*

By way of conclusion, let us return and give precision to some fundamental ideas. The Bodhisattva could not accumulate innumerable merits and thereby an inexhaustible *karma* if he were not inwardly a Buddha and freed, as such, from transgression; it is because he can no longer fall into sin or passion that the Bodhisattva gains uninterrupted merits and realizes sublime perfections; the sacrificial actions attributed to him symbolize both his transcendent virtues – the Pāramitās – and the sacrifice which his willing epousal of the samsāric condition itself represents. What distinguishes the Bodhisattva from the Buddha is, assuredly, not an inferior knowledge, but the fact of being in Samsāra, or more precisely of being there in a certain fashion and as a matter of principle. The terrestrial Buddha is distinguished from the Bodhisattvas by the fact that a celestial 'Word' is incarnate in him and that he has thus obtained the function of 'founding a religion' – to use western terms – and of emerging from transmigration thereafter; moreover the one does not go without the other, for he who has affected an 'exit' out of the world must henceforth keep watch over this Way and has no further function to exercise with regard to 'living beings'.

There are, in effect, four realities to be envisaged: Samsāra, Nirvāna, the Bodhisattva and the Buddha; the latter may be described, in his capacity of Tathāgata as 'Samsāra entered into Nirvāna', while the Bodhisattva is on the contrary and in principle 'Nirvāna present in Samsāra'. Equally it has been said that the Buddha represents the contemplative aspect and the Bodhisattva the dynamic aspect of Nirvāna, or that the former is turned towards the Absolute and the latter towards contingency. The Buddha is a ray coming forth from the Centre and returning to it, and the Bodhisattva is a circle projecting the Centre into the periphery; the Buddha illumines or saves by his radiance like the sun lighting up and warming its own planetary system; while the Bodhisattva, for his part, traces as it were a spirally converging course through Samsāra, using the very current of becoming as a means of drawing behind him the unnumbered myriads of beings till, sooner or later, they can be brought to the Centre where the wheel of existence itself does not turn and where alone felicity is to be found. Or again, the Buddha transmits Light or Knowledge 'vertically', while the Bodhisattva manifests 'horizontally' Warmth, Compassion, Mercy.

The Buddha manifests the truth that 'Samsāra is Nirvāna'; and the Bodhisattva the truth that 'Nirvāna is Samsāra'; but it could also be said that each manifests both truths after his own fashion, according to the aspect or function which is dominant in each case. This amounts to saying that Bodhisattva and Buddha alike are manifestations at once free and necessary of the very Principle of Enlightenment which some refer to the *Ādi*, or Primordial, Buddha while others personify it as Mahā-Vairōchana, 'He who operates perfect Enlightenment' according to the Tibetan rendering of the name.

CHAPTER XVI

THE FEMININE ELEMENT IN MAHĀYĀNA

'TRANSCENDENT WISDOM' (*prajnā*), the most exalted of the six spiritual disciplines (*pāramitās*) that constitute the Bodhisattvas' way, is personified in the form of a divinity bearing the name itself of Prajnāpāramitā; if man becomes wise this does in fact occur thanks to pre-existing Wisdom, whose both virginal and maternal function is the Beatitude inherent in Wisdom. This divinity is the 'Mother of all the Buddhas' and thus is not without analogy with the goddess Tārā, or more precisely with the 'White Tārā' who, for her part, is assimilated with Transcendent Wisdom. The Mongols call her 'Mother Tārā' (*Dara Eke*) and qualify her as 'Mother of all Buddhas and Bodhisattvas', while in Tibet Tārā is known as 'Saviouress' (*Dölma*). Viewed from the standpoint of her human support as also of the 'body of glory',[1] Prajnāpāramitā or Tārā can be recognized in queen Māyā, mother of the historical Buddha.

'He (the king Sākya) had a queen called Māyā, as if to say that she was free from all illusion (*māyā*); a splendour proceeding from his splendour, like the sun's magnificence when it is free from any obscuring influence; a queen supreme in the assembly of all queens. Like a mother for her subjects . . . she was the most eminent of goddesses for the whole world. – But queen Māyā having beheld the great glory of her new-born child . . . could not sustain the joy he brought to her; and so as not to die of it, she ascended to Heaven'.[2]

[1] The *Sambhoga-Kāya* or beatific body situated metaphysically between the Buddha's terrestrial body, *Nirmāna-kāya* and his divine or universal body, *Dharma-kāya*.
[2] The *Buddha-Karita* of Asvagosha (I, 15, 16 and II, 18).

According to one *Jātaka* 'the mother of a Buddha . . . is a person who has realized the perfections throughout a hundred thousand *kalpas* and who has been faithful to the five precepts from the day of her birth'.[1]

The Annunciation takes the form of "Mahā-Māyā's dream", in which she sees a glorious white elephant descending from the skies to enter her womb. . . . It is not explicitly said, but can be presumed that the birth was "virgin"; in any case it is interesting that the story was already known to Hieronymus who mentions it in a discussion on Virginity and in connection with the miraculous births of Plato and Christ'. (*Libri adv. Jovinianum* I, 42.)[2]

When it comes to the Buddha himself, he can be called a manifestation of the absolute Buddha – The Ādi-Buddha or Vajradhara or Mahāvairōchana according to the various terminologies – while his august Mother manifests the complementary power of the universal Buddha or the saving grace inherent in Nirvāna and emanating therefrom. Analogous remarks could also be made about Gopa Yashodhara, the wife of Sākyamuni and about their son Rāhula. All the nobility of this most perfect spouse is revealed in the fact that she gave herself up to lamentation, not for the simple reason that her husband Sākyamuni had left her, but because he had not taken her with him into exile in order to share in his austerities; at a later date she understood the reason for this and entered the Buddha's community.

Since 'extremes meet', it is significant that the most intellectual and ascetic and therefore, in a sense, the most virile possible attitude, namely Knowledge (*prajnāpāramitā*) should coincide with a feminine principle, as if a kind of compensatory inversion were produced at the very summit or in the ultimate depths of abstraction or extinction; in Vedantic terms one might say that *Ātmā*, inasmuch as It is perfect *Sat* and perfect *Chit*,

---

[1] Guénon has remarked that 'the mother of the Buddha is called *Māyā-Dēvī*' and that, with the Greeks and Latins, 'Maia was also the mother of Hermes and Mercury'. (*Hermes*, in *Le Voile d'Isis*, special number on *Hermetism*, spring of 1932).

[2] Ananda K. Coomaraswamy in *Hinduism and Buddhism*, chapter on *The Myth*.

Being and Knowledge, for that very reason includes *Ānanda*, Bliss, and necessarily so. Use of the symbolism of femininity may seem surprising in a Buddhist climate; it is true that these feminine symbols in the first instance refer, quite evidently, to universal realities that have nothing human about them, but the human concomitances of the symbol nonetheless remain what they are; that is to say, the immediate human significance of the image always retains its rights without there being the least danger here of irreducible contradictions or moral conflicts. Sages are the first to understand that femininity in itself is independent of earthly accidentality or of the samsārically contingent aspects of the carnal creature; if it is opportune to turn away from seductions and, in certain respects, from all attachments regardless of the nature of their supports, it is on the other hand neither possible nor desirable to escape from the *principle* of femininity, which is nirvānic in essence, that is to say divine. The, in principle, more or less a-sexual character of Mahāyāna divinities only relates to privative contingencies and does not refer to their positive substance; and furthermore, the fluctuations in the mahāyānic imagery and in its eso-exoteric interpretations indicate in their own way the complexity of all these relationships, as well as human embarrassment in the face of this complexity.

According to the greater *Sukhāvati-Vyūha* which together with the lesser *Sukhāvati-Vyūha* and the *Amitāyur-Dhyāna-sūtra* is the chief scriptural authority for the Pure Land schools, the woman who attains the paradise of Amitābha is supposed to 'despise her femininity': which means, that she is completely delivered from the physiological and psychological servitude of her earthly condition but not of her celestial substance, otherwise the power to assume a 'female form' attributed to divinities described either as masculine or as 'a-sexual' would make no sense: the harshness of the dogmatic position has its source in the sincerity of renunciation, or rather in the intention to express and to induce this sincerity. Here we have two differing perspectives that cross and mutually modify one another: according to the first view, woman is considered as the principal factor of the seduction that chains beings to Samsāra, to the point of appearing as the very genius of the latter; according to the second view, representing as it were the opposite side of the same circle, femininity is revealed on the contrary in its positive reality of maternity, virginity, beauty and mercy; it is the Christian opposition, or complementarism, between Eve and Mary. Moreover another point is important: in the face of Heaven, every creature displays a 'feminine' character and this is why it is said, in Hinduism, that every soul is a *gopi* in love with Krishna; but from the point of view of participative analogy – not of complementary opposition – every soul on the contrary has something 'masculine' about it, and it is this fact which Buddhism has in mind when it appears to wish to close Heaven to female access. This, let it be stressed once again, is independent of the consideration of the 'glorious body' of Buddhahood which is of quite another order, being a cosmic and not a spiritual question.

It should be noted in the present context that the whole *Amitāyur-Dhyāna-Sūtra* is addressed by the Buddha to a woman, the queen Vaidehī and similarly that the lesser *Sukhāvatī-Vyūha* does not omit to specify that it is addressed to women as well as men, though at first their admission into the Buddhist Order was not brought about without some difficulty. To quote the relevant passage (sections 10 and 17) from the latter scripture:

'Whatever son or daughter of a family shall hear the name of the blessed Amitāyus (an aspect of Amitābha symbolizing 'limitless life'), the Tathāgata ('He thus come'), and having heard it shall keep it in mind . . . when that son or daughter of a family comes to die, then that Amitāyus, the Tathāgata, surrounded by an assembly of disciples and followed by a host of Bodhisattvas, will stand before them at their hour of death, and they will depart this life with tranquil minds. After their death they will be born in the world Sukhāvatī, in the Buddha-country of the same Amitāyus, the Tathāgata. Therefore then, O Sāriputra . . . every son and every daughter of a family ought with their whole mind to make fervent prayers for that Buddha country.'

The same text says further on: 'Every son or daughter of a family who shall hear the name of that repetition of the Law and keep in memory the names of those blessed Buddhas, will be favoured by the Buddhas and will never return again, being once in possession of the transcendent true Knowledge'.

In certain sectors of Buddhism there exists, incontestably and even of necessity, a tendency (whether direct or indirect) to interiorize and not merely to reject femininity and sexuality, whence the occurrence of marriage within the broadly monastic framework of certain branches of the Mahāyāna as found in Tibet and Japan, which would have been unthinkable in the early days of Buddhism; the example of Shinran, the great disciple and successor of Hōnen, is particularly striking. In this connection it is also worth mentioning the visit that Hōnen received on his deathbed from queen Vaidehī, the celebrated woman disciple of the Buddha; such a supernatural happening shows that the celestial sexlessness is manifested, not in the 'glorious body', but rather in an absence of samsāric passion and in the blissfulness of inward union.

Apart from the exigencies of ascetic and disciplinary dogmatism the Buddhist a-sexualism is but a way of affirming the universal 'voidness'; one might also say that a-sexuality itself carries with it an aspect of emptiness;[1] similarly it is said of the Bodhisattva that he beholds nothing but the Void, a term which here must be understood at one and the same time in a negative or samsāric and a positive or nirvānic sense. The *Heart Sūtra*, through its spokesman the Bodhisattva Avalokiteshvara, has declared 'Where there is form, there is voidness, and where there is voidness, there is form; nor are form and voidness separable'.

One very important aspect of the symbolism of sexuality is the *upāya-prajnā* pair that figures so generally in the Vajrāyāna doctrines, represented in Tibetan iconography by two embracing divinities. It is well known that *upāya* (male and symbolized by the *vajra* or thunderbolt-sceptre) is the method or process or

[1] It is sufficiently obvious that modern views about womanhood, bound up as they are with a generalized egalitarianism and hence with a certain purely negative feminization of man as well as artificial virilization of woman, are quite out of court here. It is, however, important also to take account of a compensating phenomenon of the 'latter days' by noting the fact that piety and other spiritual gifts are more frequently to be found among women than among men.

the 'mirage' which reveals the Truth most efficaciously, whereas *prajnā* (female and symbolized by the bell) is the freedom-giving Knowledge thus revealed. This same sexual symbolism also applies in principle to the pair 'void-form' (*shūnya-rūpa*) or Nirvāna-Samsāra, since the reciprocity is analogous or even fundamentally identical. Such a symbolism may appear at first sight to be at the antipodes of the Buddhist a-sexualism; but in reality it coincides with it in the sense that in true union all polarity is out-passed and as it were annihilated in a common infinitude or in the supreme non-duality.

It is said of the Buddha that, before dying, he ascended to Heaven there to preach the Dharma to his mother Māyā; this meeting may well symbolize supreme Union inasmuch as one sees here the heavenly complement – of a positively inverse kind – of the earthly birth of the Tathāgata. This was the divine birth of Māyā in Prajnāpāramitā, Wisdom transcendent.

In order thoroughly to understand the relationship between the above imagery and the basic concepts of *upāya* and *prajnā* it is necessary to know that this second element is 'ourselves' inasmuch as it is our transpersonal essence, whereas the first-named element is the Logos which across the darkness of Samsāra awakens and actualizes THAT which we really are: every creature, as the Shingon doctrine emphatically declares, is a Buddha who does not know himself.

CHAPTER XVII

SYNTHESIS OF THE PĀRAMITĀS

WHEN one comes to consider the most conspicious thesis of the Mahāyāna, that which distinguishes it most characteristically from Theravāda Buddhism, one is inclined to think of it as a path of love, analogous to Indian *bhakti* and to Christianity taken in a general way; it is important, however, not to isolate this appearance from its complete context and to remember that the Mahāyāna essentially comprises two poles, the first being the thesis of the Bodhisattva's universal compassion while the second is the metaphysics of 'the Void', which corresponds rigorously to Advaita-Vedānta, and this, despite those differences of perspective that led to the opposition between Shankara and Nāgārjuna. Far from appearing simply as an implicit gnosis, under cover of a language attuned to a mysticism of love, this metaphysics is set forth in unmistakable terms in many *sūtras* where it calls attention to itself as being the very reason underlying the whole Mahāyāna; it governs the entire corpus of doctrine, in such a way that the initial charity becomes impregnated with it. The starting point of the way – the Bodhisattvayāna – is in fact the birth of an awareness that all things are 'void'; it is not a matter of a merely moral option. The *ego* of the aspirant thus starts off by identifying itself with the whole of Samsāra; it is through understanding the nature of the latter that the soul disengages itself from its congenital error and lays itself open to the realization of the Universal Body of the Buddha.

Before going further, we must answer a question concerning an apparently paradoxical phenomenon which seems to be peculiar to the Mahāyāna: what meaning attaches to the assertion that in the early days of Buddhism the times were not yet 'ripe' for the public preaching of the mahāyānic *sūtras* and that until then – till the time of Nāgārjuna that is to say – they had remained either secret or concealed and guarded by genii or Nāgas against all profanation? These Nāgas are depicted as serpents whose symbolism, like that of dragons, is well known in connection with the guardianship of treasures and sacred precincts. The key to the enigma lies in the fact that certain aspects of Revelation require an appropriate field of resonance; that is to say tradition plays the part, not only of communicating vital truths, but also of creating an environment adapted to the manifestation of spiritual modes of a particular character.

This is a phenomenon that occurs in some degree or other at the heart of all religions. In every religion, some few centuries after its foundation, one sees a fresh flowering or a kind of second youth, and this is due to the fact that the presence of a collective and material ambience realized by the religion itself creates conditions allowing, or requiring, an expansion of an apparently new kind: in the West, the Middle Ages with their great saints of a special type and with their chivalry and their fully developed and perfected sacred art which by that time had become a definitive and irreplaceable element, were the Christian Ages *par excellence;* they were so, moreover, in a manner different from the first centuries of Christianity which, from another point of view, clearly retain their own superiority of original perfection. Similarly, in Islam, the period of a saint like Ibn Arabi, the 'genius' of his time, coincides with a world elaborated in the course of several centuries of Islamic moulding and displays, on the esoteric plane, a very ample and profound flowering which at times verges on the initial prophetic revelation.

In Buddhism this law, or this possibility, shows itself on a scale unknown anywhere else and this it is that makes the originality of the Mahāyāna, not from the point of view of content, but as a phenomenon: far from just amounting to a perplexing enigma, this second affirming of the Buddhist revelation in reality represents a perfectly clear and limpid possibility, one that had to be manifested in its proper time and place and in all possible fullness. Under the heading of Mahāyāna the Vajrayāna or Tantrik Buddhism is also implied, which is sometimes described as a 'third setting in motion of the Wheel of Dharma' and which repeats in its own fashion, within the framework of the Mahāyāna itself, this restatement about which we have been speaking. Where the one or the other is in question, however, or even the Hīnayāna (to use Mahāyāna terminology), it is important to remember that there is no effect without a cause; by which we mean that the only possible cause of the values traditionally referred to the Buddha is the Buddha himself and no other; the homage paid to him by Brahmanists, including Shankara, is but one further indication, among many other signs, of the avatāric scope of his personality.

The better to describe the deepest purpose and meaning of the Mahāyāna, attention should be drawn to the following factors: without ever departing from its essential serenity, Buddhism, at least under one of its aspects, displays a bewilderingly quantitative character, something desperately riveted to 'horizontal' causality or to action and the gathering of merits, something strongly mysogynist moreover, if one may so express oneself: one seems to get lost in myriads of *kalpas* and in practically limitless accumulations of merit and demerit. Buddhism wishes by these means to suggest the nature of Samsāra, which is a bottomless gulf, an immeasurable system of concentric circles while being at the same time a spiroidal movement without beginning or end, or without other beginning or end than that which limits it metaphysically, namely Nirvāna, which envelops all, absorbs all, extinguishes all: evidently all this is related to the extreme precariousness of the chances of entering the human state, which is to other states as the centre to the periphery, or as a point to space. In esotericism, however, these exasperating quantities are reduced to a mere mirage while femininity is grasped in its universal essence and Deliverance becomes a lightning flash; what is thus affirmed is the truth that our Deliverance was there before us and that in an apparently insuperable difficulty there is a secret point where all becomes easy – a mystery of intellection for Zen, Shingon and Tendai and a mystery of grace for Jōdo. After numberless efforts worth no more than a gesture man is breathed in by the Heavens and 'falls upwards', as it were, into his own Deliverance; our merits carry no positive value, they merely serve to eliminate, more symbolically than effectively, the obstacles which cut us off from the heavenly Attraction.

Every spiritual cycle, whatever be its scale of magnitude, implies these alternations. On earth, Rigour is manifested before Mercy, be it only to prepare for the coming of the latter; but in the celestial spheres Mercy comes before Rigour and coincides in its substance with the blissful dimension of the Absolute itself.

*

Charity (*dāna*), which in a way constitutes the framework or the periphery of the Mahāyāna, is accounted the first of the six Pāramitās or virtues of the Bodhisattva; 'the Bodhisattva's Vow' to serve all beings great and small by a total sacrifice of self marks, for an aspirant, his formal acceptance of *dāna* as his rule of life; the Mahāyāna proper starts from this point. Wisdom (*prajnā*) is the sixth and the culmination of all the Pāramitās. The four other virtues are as it were intermediary: these are discipline (*shīla*) together with its implicit renunciation of worldly values, virility[1] (*vīrya*), patience (*kshānti*) and contemplation (*dhyāna*); these spiritual modes amount to so many paths, at once simultaneous and successive, and any single one of them can determine a whole life without needing on that account to exclude the day to day practice of the others or in fact being able to do so. The first five Pāramitās moreover are not really separated from the virtue of *prajnā*, whereof they are secondary aspects destined to contribute in their own way to the dawning of liberating Knowledge.

From the point of view of method the essence of the Mahāyāna can be summarized in the 'transfer of one's own

[1] *Shīla* can also be rendered by the word 'ethics'; from which, however, renunciation is inseparable inasmuch as any acceptance of a spiritual discipline in opposition to the pull of worldly appetites implies a reversal of direction, a 'conversion' at some degree or other. This moreover goes to show that in the order of strict logic, as distinct from the special case of the Mahāyāna, it is *shīla* that will head the list of Pāramitās with *dāna* coming in at an intermediate stage on the way to *prajnā*, which marks the goal. This alternative sequence of the six essential virtues has given its name to another work of the author's namely *Stations of Wisdom* (John Murray 1961) where it forms the subject of the final chapter. That version and the present one complete and comfirm one another; both Buddhist and non-Buddhist readers will find a comparison of the two illuminating in many ways. (*Translator's note*).

merits to others' (*parināmana*): enlightenment as well as salvation, both in the metaphysical scheme and in respect of moral intention, includes all the beings of the visible and invisible universe. If the Bodhisattva is supposed to 'refuse entry into Nirvāna so long as a single blade of grass remains undelivered', this means two things: firstly (this is the cosmic viewpoint) it means that the function of Bodhisattva coincides with what in Western language may be termed the permanent 'angelic presence' in the world, a presence which only disappears with the world itself at the final reintegration, called 'apokatastasis' in the language of Western gnosis; secondly (this is the metaphysical viewpoint) it means that the Bodhisattva, realizing the 'emptiness' of things, thereby realizes the emptiness and on the same showing the nirvānic quality of Samsāra as such. If on the one hand all is 'emptiness', on the other hand all is Nirvāna, the Buddhist notion of emptiness being at one and the same time negative and positive, as expressed in the sentence 'Form is void and Void is form'. The Samsāra, which seems at first to be inexhaustible, so that the Bodhisattva's vow appears to have something excessive or even crazy about it, becomes 'instantly' reduced – in the nontemporal instantaneity of *prajnā* – to universal Enlightenment (*Sambodhi*); on this plane, every antinomy is transcended and as it were consumed. 'Delivering the last blade of grass' amounts, in this sense, to beholding it in its nirvānic essence or to apprehending the unreality of its non-deliverance.

Since *prajnā* is the synthesis of the other five Pāramitās, the Mahāyāna is reducible in principle to *prajnā;* that is to say, the interior union with the Transcendent Void could suffice in principle for spiritual sustenance all the way. In point of fact, however, human nature is opposed to unity and simplicity and any method of regeneration will therefore have to take account of every aspect of our samsāric imprisonment; whence the necessity for a way which, while exhibiting an element of unity and simplicity from the outset, proceeds from the multiple to the one and from the complex to the simple.[1]

[1] This is what the exponents of pseudo-Zen and pseudo-Vedanta will not understand – be it said in passing – imagining, as they do, that our nature can be conjured away through mental contrivances as pretentious as they are ineffective.

It is not difficult to conceive how the five preceding virtues or spiritual methods are contained in the sixth one: to begin with, there is no possibility of gnosis without an element of renunciation or detachment; gnosis necessarily implies, in an extrinsic way, a factor of moral alternative upon which it can base itself and which allows of its expansion. Similarly, gnosis demands virility or 'heroicness': it does in fact comprise an aspect of struggle against the manifold seductions of the Samsāra, both internal and external; there is no spiritual victory without 'the fight against the dragon'. To these virtues of rigour must be added the virtues of gentleness, to wit charity and patience: the latter is by its nature the consort of re-nunciation just as charity is the consort of virility. Gnosis calls for an element of generosity and also an element of beauty, if one may so express oneself: the 'mathematical' and 'masculine' side has need of a 'musical' and 'feminine' complement, the whole universe moreover being woven from this warp and this weft; without beauty, truth cannot manifest itself faithfully according to its nature and in such fashion as to convey its complete message. If one considers the canonical image of the Buddha, the following observation can be made: if the Buddha represents renunciation then the lotus that bears him will be patience; if he represents virility, his lotus-seat will be charity; and if he is the supreme Knowledge, the lotus will be contem-plation, with all the virtues that are implied in it.

*

Pure Land Buddhism, taught in China by Tan-Luan, Tao-Cho and Shan-Tao and later in Japan by Hōnen and Shinran, in certain respects offers itself as a merciful synthesis of the six Pāramitās. Universal Enlightenment is latent in all things since everything, being 'void', is 'none other than the Void'; now this Enlightenment is able to include and in a way absorb the individual through the *upāya* of compassion represented by the remembrance of Amitābha Buddha, operated thanks to the formula *'namo' mitābhaya Buddhaya'* (in Japanese, *Namu Amida Butsu*). As spiritual realization exists 'prior to' man, the latter, who possesses no more reality of his own than foam possesses in relation to water, 'falls back' into his own pre-existing Nirvāna which, as it were, takes the initiative in its capacity of Bodhi, Enlightenment. Under these conditions, strange as this may seem, it is Nirvāna 'in act' which assumes the Pāramitās; this is what tradition calls 'power of the other' (*tariki*), in contrast with 'power of oneself' (*jiriki*), which is the predominant spiritual principle for ordinary Buddhism as also for those esotericisms that function apart from the cult of Amitābha, such as Zen or Shingon in Japan: we have to say 'predominant', since neither principle can be totally absent, each is to be found latent in the other, as required by the all-overriding principle of 'non-duality' whereof the Taoist emblem of *yin-yang* provides a most telling symbolical illustration.

This celestial gift of the Pāramitās flowering in advance, or this saving grace granted in function of the prior realization of these virtues by Amitābha (himself a projection at one and the same time of universal Buddhahood and of the historical Buddha) – this heavenly gift, as we have said, is comprised in the 'original Vow' of the Buddha, the cosmic or divine act on which the whole Pure Land doctrine is really built. Participation by the faithful in the Pāramitās is then essentially reducible to faith, in which three aspects or mental states are distinguishable, namely 'truthful thought' or 'a sincere spirit', 'profoundly believing thought' and 'the wish to be reborn in the Pure Land'. According to the *Amitayur-Dhyāna-sūtra*, 22, the first-named state excludes all dissimulation and all lukewarmness; the second state, according to Hōnen, implies on the one hand a consciousness of our own misery and incapacity and, on the other hand, a consciousness of the saving power of Amitābha and of his wish to save us if only we call on him with faith. The third mental state means that we offer up all our merits in the sole intention of being born in the Pure Land and that by the same token we take pleasure, within the framework of that intention, in the merits of others as if those others are ourselves, an attitude which confers on our own way a secret radiance and a kind of impersonal amplitude.

It should also be noted that there are forty-eight vows (*pranidhānas*) whereof only the eighteenth may be called the 'Original Vow'; Hōnen describes it as the 'king of vows' and it runs as follows:

'When I shall have attained the state of a Buddha, if the beings of the ten regions (of the universe) shall have believed in me with calm thoughts and shall have wished to be born in my Country and shall have thought of me be it only ten times – if these beings are not to be reborn there, then let me not obtain the perfect Knowledge; none are excepted save those who shall have committed the five mortal sins and shall have blasphemed the Good Law'.[1]

The words 'ten times' in the above text also bear a meaning of 'ten modes', such as thought, speech, vision, gesture.

However, the Pāramitās are not a matter only of mental attitudes, they are above all inherent in the 'remembrance of Buddha' (*buddhānusmriti*) itself:[2] this is the same as saying that the perpetual remembrance of the Buddha is at the same time renouncement or purity, virility or persevering activity, patience or peace, generosity or fervour, contemplation or discernment, wisdom or union. In fact to keep oneself in this remembrance alone, or in the act that fixes this remembrance in temporal duration thus reducing the latter to an eternal instant, goes not without renunciation of the world and of oneself, and this allows one to understand at the same time the part played here by the Pāramitā of virility: if renunciation (by way of discipline, *shīla*) is a participation in Eternity, virility (*vīrya*), for its part, will place itself under the sign of the Eternal Present, like the lightning or the 'third eye'. As for patience (*kshānti*), this consists (within the context of remembrance) in dwelling quietly at the Centre, in the grace of Amitābha, while charity (*dāna*) is on the contrary a projecting of one's *ego* into the distance, or the extending of one's will beyond the enclosing shell of individuality: if patience is founded in our consciousness of possessing all things in grace, charity will be our consciousness of living in all things and extending

---

[1] The greater *Sukhāvatī-Vyūha-sūtra* VIII, 18, according to the Chinese translation, the surviving Sanskrit text being incomplete.

[2] It should be pointed out here that the Tibetan invocatory formula *Om mani padme hum*, though differing in its form, in virtue of its homage to the 'Jewel' and the 'Lotus' is equivalent to the Japanese *Namu Amida Butsu* and its Sanskrit prototype; in effect it is addressed to the Bodhisattva Avalokiteshvara and for that reason also to the Buddha Amitābha whose emanation he is.

our spiritual activity to the whole of creation. The remembrance of Amitābha also implies, with all the more reason, the virtues of contemplation (*dhyāna*) and Knowledge (*prajnā*); the latter corresponds in a sense to Plenitude and the former to the Void. Previously it was pointed out that 'the Void' bears both a negative and a positive meaning; it is to its positive meaning that the name of 'Plenitude' can be given. The Void is Plenitude inasmuch as it is opposable to the 'nothingness' of Samsāra, not inasmuch as it is its Quintessence, for in the latter respect all is Plenitude and all is Voidness.

It would be possible to express this teaching still more simply by saying that the synthesis of the Pāramitās is realized in the most evident way by the two indispensable conditions of the *nembutsu*, namely 'faith' and 'action': the latter sums up the active virtues and the former the contemplative virtues, both of which moreover include some static and some dynamic elements, such as abstention in the case of action and ardour in the case of faith. Furthermore, the two above categories bring us to the twin pillars of all spirituality, namely 'discernment' and 'concentration', or doctrine and method. In fact, all possible qualities whether intellectual, psychic or moral, find their place under these two denominations, since they must needs derive either from intelligence or from the will and thus describe, through indicating what we ought to be, what we really are in our innate and eternal Buddhahood.

*

According to a special symbolism much used in the Mahāyāna, the Universal or Dhyāni Buddhas, also called Jinas or Victorious Ones, came forth by projection from the Ādi-Buddha: they are five in number and each rules over a cardinal point, with the most eminent among them, Vairōchana, occupying the centre.[1] To Vairōchana analogically there corresponds the element Ether; to Akshobhya, the Immovable One, who rules over the East, the element Air is referred; to

[1] According to the various schools, it is Vairōchana, or Vajradhara, or Amitābha who corresponds to the Supreme; many other fluctuations in the above symbolism could be pointed out, especially where the quaternary is duplicated or multiplied and accompanied by its corresponding Bodhisattvas and Female Consorts.

Amitābha, boundless Light, there corresponds the Western direction and the element Water; to Amoghasiddhi, 'Realizer of the Aim', the North and the element Earth are allotted; while to Ratnasambhava, 'Producer of the Gem,' belong the South and the element Fire. Now Ether is everywhere, it is central and immutable in all circumstances, like truth or contemplation; the sun rises in the East, like a sword drawn from its scabbard, it is invincible and so is the air which is unchained in the hurricane; the West indicates rest and the same holds good for Water which gathers itself calmly together and endures all things; the North is cold like purity, Earth is steady like renunciation; while the South possesses the warmth of life, it is generous like charity. The *Ādi* or Primordial Buddha – or Prajñāparamitā – is symbolically placed at the Zenith, or beyond space; in relation to the sensible elements, including ether, the Ādi-Buddha rules over the supra-sensible element, namely consciousness, which means that it is to be identified, not with cosmic principles or, to be more precise, with relative knowledge as in the case of the Dhyāni-Buddhas[1], but with absolute Knowledge which envelopes all relativities even while residing beyond them.

In the esotericism of Shingon, the spread fan of the five elements folds together in 'Consciousness', regarded as a sixth and superior element: to be Buddha is to know entirely the nature of seemingly external phenomena, and therefore to know that they are not of a substance other than our own selves. To state that the Bodhisattva sees nothing but' the Void' (*shūnya*) means that he only sees the 'emptiness' (*shūnyatā*) of things, or that he sees things in their suchness which is identical with the suchness of consciousness. This vision of the emptiness of things is moreover not unnconnected with the fact that a man of noble nature sees the essential in every phenomenon, whereas the man of base nature only looks at what is accidental; now the essence of things coincides with their emptiness in the sense that it provides an opening towards the unmanifest, or itself manifests an archetype. As for the elements, they are like the external diversification or like the crystallized aspects of that unique

---

[1] Who correspond to the four archangels of Islam, with Vairōchana, at the Centre, as the equivalent of *Er-Ruh*, Spirit.

consciousness; he who looks on the world, sees himself and he who realizes that which dwells in the depths of his own heart, contains the world. The synthesis of the five objective elements in the sixth, which is subjective, prefigures in its own way the spiritual synthesis of the Pāramitās: that is to say earth, water, air, fire and ether – taken in the widest sense – are in fact the external and cosmic appearances of the first five Pāramitās while the sixth element, *chitta* or consciousness, similarly is the natural prefiguration of the sixth virtue, *prajnā*.[1] An analogous synthesis is realized in Zen, where the way consists in discovering the infinite suchness of the heart and in realizing by this means, as in a lightning flash, 'that which is'.

Let us, however, return to the synthesis operated thanks to Amitābha's vow: this bespeaks a particular relationship, not only with the symbolism of the west, the setting sun and the element water, but also, by the same token, with the virtue of patience; at the same time this perspective of a 'bhaktic' esotericism (one which, however, at its kernel does not exclude the most profound gnosis) identifies Amitābha with the Ādi-Buddha in such fashion that this symbolism of the evening coolness, as also the virtue of patience, receives thereby a preponderant and, in some sort, central meaning, that of confident self-abandonment to the 'power of the Other' and to saving Grace – an attitude which in effect derives from the nature of water and of 'passive Perfection', to borrow a Taoist term.

For the man whose heart is content to rest in the supernatural certitude of saving Grace nothing remains, humanly speaking, but to await the exhausting of his karmic effects; he is patient under the weight of whatever Samsāra has still in store for him and which is in process of being exhausted like his own earthly destiny. This perfection of confidence or quietude quite evidently could not be a pure and simple passivity; that is to say, it would amount to nothing did it not include, essentially, its complementary aspects of activity and impassibility. Each Pāramitā is like a mirror that reflects objects yet never ceases

[1] Esoterically, the lotus on which the Buddha is enthroned represents innate and latent knowledge, while his halo expresses the effective Knowledge realized by the Tathāgata.

to be itself; there is in fact no such thing as a spiritual patience without its accompaniment of renunciation and strength. This can be gathered without any shadow of doubt from the Amidist texts, such as these words of the illustrious Hōnen:[1] 'The countenance of the man who longs for Paradise and fixes his whole mind on the object of reaching it will appear as if he had a hatred and even abhorrence of the world'. – 'Again as to the passage (in Shan-Tao's book) "with a heart as strong as adamant, which is neither moved, confused nor discomfited" ... the meaning is, not to allow your merit (i.e. the benefic forces emanating from the accumulation of past merits, one's good *karma*) to be directed this way or that ... Seeing that adamant is a substance which cannot be broken, it is used by way of parable, to show the heart should not be broken in its purpose either.'

---

[1] *Honen the Buddhist Saint* (Kyoto, 1949), Vol. III, chapter XXI 8 and XXII 10.

INDEX

Absolute, the, 21, 26, 32 f., 37, 39, 41, 43 ff., 47, 49 f., 55, 57, 73, 123 ff., 128, 133 ff., 138, 146, 155, 156
Adam, 97 f., 102
'Adamantine Vehicle' (Vayrayāna), 26–8
Ādi-Buddha, 127, 133, 138, 144, 146, 148, 161 ff.
air, 161–2
Akshobhya, 161
Amaterasu-Omikami, 93 f., 97, 99 f., 102 f., 105, 107
Ame-no-Minakanushi-no-Kami, 89, 93, 104
Amida, 105, 117, 122
Amitābha, 19, 21 f., 26, 56, 105, 117, 122, 131, 133 f., 149 f., 163
Amitāyur-Dhyāna-Sūtra, 149 f., 158
Amoghasiddhi, 162
Ānanda, 149
anātmā, doctrine of, 39, 65
ancestors, worship of, 85–8, 91, 103, 108
anthropomorphism, 19 ff.
Apocatastasis, 135, 143, 157
Archangels, 134, 138 f., 162
archery, 74
art, Buddhist, 20, 75 f., 109, 111 f., 119 ff., 123
atheism, 18 f., 22
Atmā, 26, 65, 93, 124, 148

Being, 21, 27, 31, 37, 49, 57 f., 63, 93, 119, 136, 138, 149
Bhagavadgita, the, 62
Boddhidharma, 26, 75
Bodhi, 66, 139, 141, 144, 159
Bodhisattvas, 18, 21 82, 108, 117, 121, 129 ff., 140 ff., 150 f., 152, 156, 161
body, resurrection of, 61
Buddha, 17 ff., 21, 24 ff., 31, 49, 53, 60, 66 f., 72, 74, 119, 122 ff., 132, 134, 136 ff., 144 ff., 151 f., 154,

158, 162; images of, 20, 24, 26, 117, 119, 120–1, 157; person of, 24–6; teaching of, 24 f., 66, 120; terrestrial, 138, 140, 141, 142, 145, 146, 147; *see also* Ādi-Buddha, Akshobhya, Amitābha, Amoghasiddhi, Mahāvairōchana, Ratnasambhava, Vairōchana
Buddhas, 21, 49, 128 ff., 144, 161
Buddha-hood, universal, 28, 37, 43, 67 f., 73, 119 f., 124, 135, 159
Buddhi, 26, 93, 124

caste, 92
charity, 29–32, 126, 129 ff., 136, 139, 153, 156, 158, 160, 162
China, 19, 81, 107, 117, 122 f., 131, 136, 158
Christ, 21, 25, 49, 57, 67, 94, 132
Christianity, 20, 28 f., 49, 52, 55, 60, 62, 67, 77, 91, 96, 109 f., 112, 122, 126, 128, 145, 150, 153
compassion, 56, 128, 130, 132, 134 f., 143, 145, 146, 153, 158
Confucianism, 50, 85, 92
consciousness, 43, 54 f., 57 f., 60, 71, 87, 91, 160, 162 f.
contemplation, 20, 44, 125 ff., 133, 136, 146, 156, 158, 160 ff.
contemplatives, 124–7, 139
cosmology, 46 f., 89
Cosmos, 26 f., 37, 39 ff., 48 f., 56 f., 64, 68, 93 f., 104, 138
creation, 27, 47, 62, 144, 161

damnation, 50, 54
dead, veneration of, 85
death, 22, 42, 49, 61 ff., 104, 133, 136 f., 150
death penalty, 30
deliverance, 24, 28, 45, 49 f., 66, 133
destiny, *see* karma
Dharma, the, 20, 24, 76 f., 119, 122, 133, 137, 141, 142, 143, 152, 155